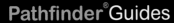

Country Walks near London

Escape the city for glorious rural walks

Walks selected by
Nick Channer

Contents

Country Walks near London

If you live in London you may feel that planning a day's walking in the country is something of an onerous task. Where are the best routes and by what means do you get to them? The answers lie in this dedicated Pathfinder® Guide.

True, walking involves a certain amount of planning but it's easier than you think. There is a wide variety of good walks within easy reach of London, as the choice in this guide demonstrates, and in this increasingly climate-conscious world of ours, the ideal way to do it is to combine a country walk with an environmentally friendly train journey. In other words, forget the stress of traffic congestion, leave the car at home and use public transport.

All London's main line stations provide regular services to the country and all the walks in this book can be reached by train. By letting the train take the strain you can relax and enjoy the view on the way. Travelling by this mode of transport to begin your walk should be much more than a means of getting from A to B. As a nation we have always loved trains and train travel and this is reflected in some of our best-loved literature.

Sir Arthur Conan Doyle's legendary detective Sherlock Holmes frequently travelled around the country by train. In *The Adventure of the Retired Colourman*, Conan Doyle describes a train journey from Liverpool Street to the Frinton area of Essex (*Walk 2*).

Agatha Christie loved train travel and regularly travelled from Paddington through Streatley and Goring (*Walks 24 and 27*) to her home in the Thames Valley. John Betjeman was also passionate about trains and in his television film *Metroland*, made in 1973, he travels on the Metropolitan Line to leafy Buckinghamshire (Chesham, *Walk 26*). Passengers can still make that same journey today, passing through Betjeman's beloved Metroland to the heart of the country.

Combining walks and train travel represents a package, an experience. Even today, for many people there is still a hint of adventure, a sense of nostalgia about a train journey – however short. There is nothing better or more worthwhile than escaping the city by train and enjoying the numerous benefits of a walk in the country.

For general enquiries about trains call the National Rail Enquiry Line on 08457 484950.

1 *Northchurch Common & the Grand Union Canal*

Canal towpath, grassy tracks, residential roads and lanes

 6 miles (9.7km)

🕐 3 hours

2 *The Naze and Walton Channel*

Promenade, shore paths and local roads

🚶 6 miles (9.7km)

 2½ hours

3 *Aldbury, Ivinghoe Beacon and Ashridge*

Good field and woodland paths and tracks

 7¾ miles (12.4km)

 3½ hours

4 *Stour Valley: Constable Country*

Field paths, tracks and riverside paths

 7½ miles (12.1km)

🕐 3½ hours

5 *White Notley and Cressing*

Tracks, field paths and quiet lanes

🚶 9½ miles (15.3km)

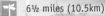 4½ hours

6 *Newport and Debden*

Tracks, fields and parkland paths, and lanes

🚶 6½ miles (10.5km)

🕐 3 hours

Finchingfield

Hertfordshire & Essex

On the cliffs at The Naze

North and north east of London lies a vast, essentially English landscape that is the epitome of the Home Counties. Hertfordshire and neighbouring Essex may lack the dramatic downland of the South Downs and the stunning beechwoods of the Chilterns, but they have a gentle beauty and a surprisingly varied wealth of striking features and tourist attractions. Dedham and the Stour Valley, on the Essex/Suffolk border, are popular with walkers and cyclists. The artist John Constable spent much of his early life sketching here.

Another Essex gem beloved of walkers, though rarely heard of outside the county boundary, is the Brain Valley, between Witham and Braintree. This secluded corner of Essex has changed little over the years and the many splendid churches in the area stand as grand monuments to the past.

Much of Essex is famously flat but the area around the villages of Newport and Debden, east of the M11 and just south of Saffron Walden, is surprisingly hilly and undulating. Again, some of the county's historic churches form part of an ever-changing scenic backdrop.

The Essex coast is a marvellous geological feature of the county and in stark contrast to its rural hinterland. Here, meandering creeks and estuaries drift towards the North Sea and coastal footpaths thread their lonely way beneath wide skies and beside endless marshes and mudflats. Walton-on-the-Naze, a popular seaside resort, is a good base for walking and birdwatching.

Across the Essex border in Hertfordshire numerous walks reflect the county's distinctive character and diversity. For example, the Grand Union Canal at Berkhamsted – birthplace of the writer Graham Greene – offers the chance to walk into Britain's industrial past and learn about the fascinating culture of our inland waterways.

To the north walkers are drawn to Ivinghoe Beacon, one of the highest points in the Chilterns. South of here is the vast Ashridge Estate, owned by the National Trust. With its miles of waymarked trails, Ashridge is a perfect example of how the Trust, Britain's largest landowner, has made large swathes of the countryside accessible to walkers.

Northchurch Common and the Grand Union Canal

walk 1

Start
Berkhamsted Station.
Approx. 35 minutes
from London Euston

Distance
6 miles (9.7km)

Height gain
395 feet (120m)

Approximate time
3 hours

Route terrain
Canal towpath, grassy
tracks and residential
roads and lanes

OS maps
Explorer 181 (Chiltern
Hills North)

GPS waypoints
SP 993 081
Ⓐ SP 992 082
Ⓑ SP 978 095
Ⓒ SP 970 106
Ⓓ SP 965 097

This is the first of two walks in this guide that takes you across part of the National Trust's Ashridge Estate. From Berkhamsted the route heads up onto the expanses of Northchurch Common, a superb combination of open grassland and thick woodland with fine views over the Bulbourne Valley. The return is a relaxing stroll beside the Grand Union Canal.

Berkhamsted lies in a valley that has always been a major routeway through the Chilterns from London to the Midlands and North – the Grand Union Canal, a busy railway line and a main road pass through it. The Normans recognised Berkhamsted's strategic importance and built the castle; much of the later stonework of this once important fortress and royal residence has vanished to reveal the 11th-century earthworks of the original, simple motte-and-bailey construction. Berkhamsted also has a large 13th-century church and, despite much modern development, retains some attractive old cottages.

Northchurch Common

Grand Union Canal near Berkhamsted

From the railway station, turn left, in the Ashridge and Potten End direction, to pass under a railway bridge – Berkhamsted Castle is to the right – turn left into Bridgewater Road and take the first road on the right (Castle Hill Avenue) **Ⓐ**. Head uphill and where the road bends left, keep ahead, at a public footpath sign, along an enclosed path.

Bear left along a road and at a public footpath sign, bear right along a track. At a fork, take the right-hand track, keep ahead at a public footpath sign, take the right-hand track at the next fork and continue up to climb a stile. Walk along the left edge of a field, go through a kissing-gate, continue along an enclosed path and go through a kissing-gate to a crossways. Keep ahead along an enclosed track in front of houses to a fork on the edge of woodland and take the left-hand tarmac track, heading downhill through trees. Where the track bends sharply left, keep ahead across grass and continue uphill **Ⓑ** along a grassy ride through the woodlands of Northchurch Common.

Cross a tarmac track, keep ahead, bear slightly left on emerging into an open area and follow a clear grassy track to a road. Cross over, continue

along the undulating path opposite and after a waymarked post, cross a track and keep ahead along a broad green ride. Keep ahead at a crossways and on emerging into a large open area of grassland, turn left along its left edge. At a crossways in the corner of this grassy area, 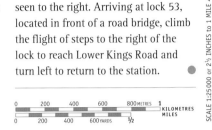 **C** turn left and on emerging from the trees, keep ahead downhill along a narrow lane. Take the first lane on the right – this is even narrower – follow it around a left bend, cross a railway bridge and continue to a T-junction.

Turn left parallel to the canal and at the next T-junction, turn right to cross a bridge and turn left onto the towpath of the Grand Union Canal **D**. Follow the towpath for just over two miles back to Berkhamsted, passing several locks, and later the little River Bulbourne is seen to the right. Arriving at lock 53, located in front of a road bridge, climb the flight of steps to the right of the lock to reach Lower Kings Road and turn left to return to the station.

SCALE 1:25000 or 2½ INCHES to 1 MILE 4CM to 1KM

walk 2

The Naze and Walton Channel

Start

Walton-on-the-Naze Station. Approx. 1 hour 40 minutes from London Liverpool Street

Distance

6 miles (9.7km)

Height gain

80 feet (25m)

Approximate time

2½ hours

Route terrain

Promenade, shore paths and local roads

OS maps

Explorer 184 (Colchester)

GPS waypoints

TM 251 214
Ⓐ TM 258 222
Ⓑ TM 266 244
Ⓒ TM 250 248
Ⓓ TM 258 228

Following the North Sea shore, the first part of this exhilarating walk of wide vistas is along the cliffs of The Naze. You then turn away from the sea and continue along the top of an embankment above creeks, marshes, mudflats and inlets to the edge of the small resort of Walton-on-the-Naze.

The word 'naze' comes from an old English for 'nose' and refers to the original shape of the headland. The high but crumbly cliffs – constantly being eaten away by the sea – are a rarity on the generally flat Essex coast.

Out of the station, turn right onto The Parade and follow its winding course along the seafront leading onto Prince's Esplanade and, just beyond the turning for the swimming pool, bear right into East Terrace Ⓐ signed for the Maritime Museum. Pass this and continue along the seafront path above a long line of beach huts. Walk the length of Cliff Parade and along the ensuing path to Naze Park Road; turn right and right again into Sunny Point. Keep ahead through a parking area to join a track leading to the Naze Tower, built in 1720 by Trinity House as a landmark. Continue northwards across the grassy clifftop, heeding the warning notices to keep well clear of the

Creeks near The Naze

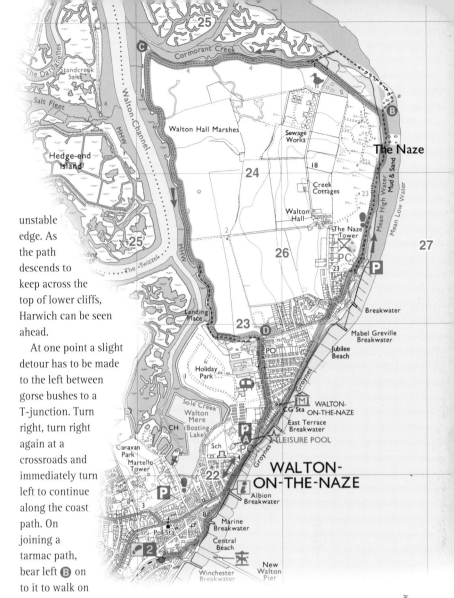

unstable edge. As the path descends to keep across the top of lower cliffs, Harwich can be seen ahead.

At one point a slight detour has to be made to the left between gorse bushes to a T-junction. Turn right, turn right again at a crossroads and immediately turn left to continue along the coast path. On joining a tarmac path, bear left **B** on to it to walk on top of an embankment, above pools and marshes and along the edge of an Essex Wildlife Trust nature reserve. Where this tarmac path ends, bear left again to continue along a pleasant grassy path – still on the top of an embankment – above Cormorant Creek and the surrounding marshland. The Naze Tower stands out prominently on the skyline to the left.

The path bends sharp left **C** to keep by the broader expanses of Walton Channel on the right and above Walton Hall Marshes on the left. A few yards before reaching a track in front of a caravan park, turn left and continue above a small pool on the right. Keep ahead and in a short while the path bends right to emerge on to a road on the edge of Walton-on-the-Naze **D**.

Turn right, all the way down Hall Lane to reach **A** and follow the seafront route back to the start. ●

SCALE 1:25000 or 2½ INCHES to 1 MILE 4CM to 1KM

walk 3

Start

Tring Station.
Approx. 45 minutes
from London Euston

Distance

7¾ miles (12.4km)

Height gain

870 feet (265m)

Approximate time

3½ hours

Route terrain

Good field and
woodland paths
and tracks

OS maps

Explorer 181 (Chiltern
Hills North)

GPS waypoints

SP 950 122
Ⓐ SP 954 124
Ⓑ SP 955 148
Ⓒ SP 960 163
Ⓓ SP 959 168
Ⓔ SP 963 155
Ⓕ SP 970 131

Aldbury, Ivinghoe Beacon and Ashridge

This outstanding walk proceeds along the Chiltern escarpment to Ivinghoe Beacon – one of the highest viewpoints in the Chilterns – and returns through part of the magnificent woodlands of the National Trust's Ashridge Estate via the picturesque village of Aldbury. There are several climbs but the paths are good, the route easy to follow, and the views superb all the way.

Exit the station pull-in, cross the main road to the pavement and turn right. Follow Station Road for about 400 yds to a Ridgeway signpost bearing left along the driveway to Westland Farm. Keep ahead where this leads left to the farmhouse to reach a crossways of tracks Ⓐ. Follow the Ridgeway left on a clear, tree-lined and gently rising track. At a path junction bear right to climb more steeply following the acorn symbol Ridgeway waymarks over Pitstone Hill. Initially the route passes through woodland, but after climbing a stile, it continues over open downland with some fine views to the left over the Vale of Aylesbury, even though the dominant feature is Pitstone Cement Works. The path later descends and curves gradually to the right, keeping close to a wire fence on the right, finally bearing left to a stile in front of Pitstone Hill car park. On this descent the escarpment and next part of the route can be seen stretching ahead to Ivinghoe Beacon.

Climb the stile, pass through the car park Ⓑ, cross a lane and take the path opposite that heads straight across a large field. Climb another stile and continue across the next field. The path then keeps below a bank on the right, ascending and curving left to a stile. Do not climb it but pass to the left of it and head across, keeping parallel to a hedge and wire fence on the right, to a Ridgeway marker post on the edge of woodland. Continue through the trees and on emerging from them keep ahead downhill, by a wire fence on the right. Turn right over a stile in the fence, head uphill through an area of scrub and bushes, and then continue downhill to climb a stile. Bear left down to the corner of a road Ⓒ. Cross the road and follow the left-hand one of the two tracks ahead up to the summit of Ivinghoe Beacon, marked by a triangulation pillar Ⓓ. This outlying spur of the Chiltern range, 764ft (233m) high, gives a magnificent panorama over the Vale of Aylesbury, along the Chiltern escarpment from Dunstable Downs to Coombe Hill and across

SCALE 1:25000 or 2½ INCHES to 1 MILE 4CM to 1KM

to the slopes of Ashridge Park.

Retrace your steps to the road
C, cross over and then turn left,
at a National Trust marker post,
along a pleasant path that
initially keeps parallel to the
road on the left, heading uphill
between trees to join a track.
Bear left along the track, which
curves left to reach an open
grassy area beside the road.
Turn right alongside hedges
on the right, parallel to the
road, and at the end of
this grassy area turn

Looking towards Ivinghoe Beacon

right **E** along a track signposted 'Ashridge Estate. Restricted access, Clipper Down Cottage only' and waymarked with a National Trust green horseshoe bridlepath waymark, which is the waymark to follow for the next mile or so.

Almost the whole of the remainder of the walk is through part of the splendid beech woods of the Ashridge Estate, over 4,000 acres of open grassland, commons and woodlands belonging to the National Trust. Follow the track through this attractive woodland, taking care to keep on the main track all the while, to Clipper Down Cottage. Go through a gate, at a Bridgewater Monument sign, pass to the right of the cottage and continue along another track: at intervals there are superb views to the right from these wooded slopes across the flatter country of the vale. Pass to the left of a log cabin and soon after crossing a footbridge you reach the Bridgewater Monument **F**, erected in 1832 in memory of the third Duke of Bridgewater, the great canal builder and owner of Ashridge. The view from the top is well worth the climb.

Keep ahead past the monument to join a track in front of the National Trust shop, information centre and tearoom. Turn right and follow the track downhill through woodland; a gap on the right reveals a superb view of Aldbury village. At a fork take the right-hand lower track to continue downhill to a road and turn right for a short distance to find the centre of Aldbury village.

All the ingredients that make up the classic English village scene are present in Aldbury: charming brick and half-timbered cottages (some thatched) and a pub grouped around a triangular green; duck pond, stocks and whipping-post standing on the green; and a short distance away a medieval church. The village is set against the backdrop of the beech woods of Ashridge. Aldbury has frequently been used as a film set.

Continue along Toms Hill Road at the meeting of several lanes and just beyond the churchyard corner go right, through a kissing-gate, along a waymarked field path. Pass the buildings of Church Farm, left, and follow the ongoing hedged pathway dividing two large fields to a track intersection. Turn left to reach **A** and retrace your outward route to return to Tring Station. ●

Stour Valley: Constable Country

This classic walk is in the Stour Valley on the Essex–Suffolk border, immortalised in the paintings of John Constable. An undulating route along the well-waymarked Essex Way, mainly via tracks and field paths, brings you to Dedham. The walk then continues by the winding River Stour through Dedham Vale, the heart of Constable Country, passing the landmarks of Flatford Mill and Willy Lott's Cottage before returning to the start. Pick a fine day and take time to enjoy this outstanding walk to the full.

Start
Manningtree Station. Approx. 1 hour 10 minutes from London Liverpool Street

Distance
7½ miles (12.1km)

Height gain
245 feet (75m)

Approximate time
3½ hours

Route terrain
Field paths, tracks and riverside paths

OS maps
Explorer 196 (Sudbury, Hadleigh & Dedham Vale)

GPS waypoints
- TM 094 322
- Ⓐ TM 092 321
- Ⓑ TM 080 315
- Ⓒ TM 066 318
- Ⓓ TM 059 319
- Ⓔ TM 057 331
- Ⓕ TM 057 336
- Ⓖ TM 067 337
- Ⓗ TM 075 333

With your back to the station building, head diagonally right through the car park and take the path, signposted to Flatford and Dedham, down to a T-junction and turn right along a tree-lined track. At a footpath post, turn left Ⓐ in the Lawford church direction, along an enclosed path, which heads steadily uphill, bends right and then left to reach the church.

Go through a gate into the churchyard, pass to the right of the church and the path bears left to exit the churchyard by another gate. Head across to public footpath and Essex Way signs, bear right to a field corner and continue into trees to a kissing-gate. Go through and head diagonally right to go through another one. Turn left along the straight, tarmac track, pass beside a gate and turn right along a road.

Follow the road around a left-hand bend and after ¼ mile, bear left Ⓑ at a public bridleway sign, along an enclosed track to a gate. Go through, continue along the enclosed track and turn left through a gate. Walk along a track, passing to the left of a cottage, and bear left on joining another track. Follow the track around a right-hand bend, keep ahead at a crossroads and the track bears right down to a farm. At an Essex Way sign, bear right off the track, walk across grass to enter woodland and continue gently downhill to cross a plank footbridge.

Climb a stile, keep ahead across a field to climb another, carefully cross a railway line, climb a stile and go through a kissing-gate and keep straight ahead across a field to another kissing-gate. Go through and keep ahead between fences to go through a further kissing-gate. Continue along an enclosed path to a road. Cross over, go through the kissing-gate opposite, bear slightly left across a field to the corner and climb a stile on to a lane.

Turn right and the lane curves left and continues through trees. Where it bends right, keep ahead  through a kissing-gate, head gently uphill along the left-hand edge of a field to go through a gate, and keep ahead over the brow to go through another kissing-gate later followed by a gate. Walk along an enclosed grassy path, go through a kissing-gate and continue across the middle of the next field, then along an enclosed path. In the corner, go through a gate and keep ahead along a track to a road. Turn right, at a public footpath sign turn left ⒟ over a stile and walk across a field, heading down into woodland. Climb a stile and keep along the bottom, inside edge of the wood, turning left to pass in front of a house.

Turn right along a drive to a tarmac track, turn right, passing cottages, and at a public footpath sign, turn left along a tarmac track between more cottages. Go through a gate, pass in front of a farmhouse, turn right through another gate and keep ahead to a stile. After climbing it, walk along the left-hand edge of a field, go through a gate, cross a plank footbridge, bear right and head diagonally across the next field. Cross a plank footbridge and climb a stile in the corner, head across two fields, going through a kissing-gate and continue along a right-hand field edge.

In the field corner, keep ahead to climb a stile into a sports field and turn right along its right-hand edge, passing behind the cricket pavilion, to a tarmac path. Turn left along the tree-lined path, passing beside a barrier to emerge on to a road in the centre of Dedham ⒠.

From the 14th to the 17th centuries this small town was a flourishing centre of the cloth trade and has a wealth of attractive buildings. The large 'wool church' was built in 1492 and has an imposing west tower. Constable attended the local grammar school.

Keep ahead along Mill Lane, passing Dedham Mill and cross bridges over first a channel, then the main River Stour and finally another channel, here briefly entering Suffolk. At a public footpath sign to East Bergholt and Flatford, turn right ⒡ through a kissing-gate and walk across riverside meadows beside the Stour, later bearing away from the river

to a kissing-gate on the far side of the meadow. Keep ahead along a tree-lined path to a T-junction, turn sharp right **G** on to another tree-lined path and go through a kissing-gate to cross Fen Bridge over the Stour, here re-entering Essex.

Turn left down steps and go through another kissing-gate. Now comes a delightful part of the walk as you continue across meadows by the winding river through a typical Constable landscape. After going through a kissing-gate in front of a wooden footbridge **H** the route continues to the right, still beside the river, but it is worthwhile crossing the bridge to Bridge Cottage and turning right along a lane for a short distance to see Flatford Mill and Willy Lott's Cottage.

All these National Trust properties feature in Constable's paintings. Bridge Cottage houses a Constable exhibition and has a pleasant tearoom. Both Flatford Mill and Willy Lott's Cottage are leased to the Field Studies Council and are not open to the public. Constable's father owned Flatford Mill and others in the Stour Valley.

After turning right in front of the footbridge, at a public footpath sign to Manningtree, walk along a tree-lined path, passing Flatford Lock. A little farther on is a fine view across the river of Flatford Mill. Continue along the path and later you pass to the right of a concrete barrier. Cross a bridge over a channel by a lock, go through a kissing-gate and keep ahead beside the barrier to another kissing-gate. Turn left through it and walk along the top of a low embankment above pastures and marshland. Go through two more kissing-gates and, just after the second one, turn right at a public footpath sign to Manningtree station.

Go through another kissing-gate and along an enclosed path that turns first left and then right, widens into a track and passes under a railway bridge. Just beyond the bridge, turn left along a tree-lined track parallel to the embankment, which leads back to the start. ●

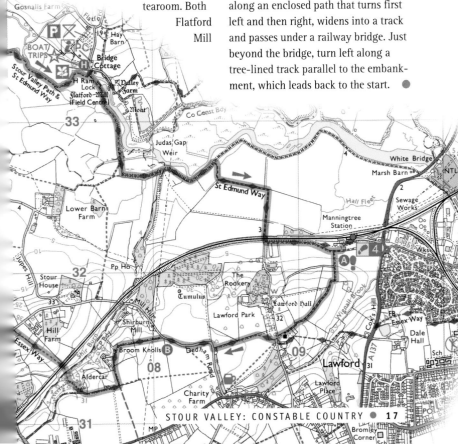

walk 5

Start

Cressing Station.
Approx. 1 hour from
London Liverpool
Street

Distance

9½ miles (15.3km)

Height gain

425 feet (130m)

Approximate time

4½ hours

Route terrain

Tracks, field paths and
quiet lanes

OS maps

Explorers 183
(Chelmsford & The
Rodings) and 195
(Braintree & Saffron
Walden

GPS waypoints

TL 776 202
Ⓐ TL 781 201
Ⓑ TL 772 195
Ⓒ TL 783 185
Ⓓ TL 787 184
Ⓔ TL 799 185
Ⓕ TL 788 201
Ⓖ TL 792 209
Ⓗ TL 778 211

White Notley and Cressing

This is a lengthy but relatively undemanding walk, mainly along well-signed tracks, field paths and quiet lanes, in the pleasant countryside of the Brain Valley to the south of Braintree. It passes through two attractive villages, both with traditional Essex churches, and includes a detour to the interesting Cressing Temple. A shorter version omits this detour.

Turn right out of the parking area to go over the level-crossing and walk along the lane to a T-junction. Turn right, in the Witham direction, and at a public footpath sign just before a farm Ⓐ, turn sharp right over a stile and walk along the right-hand edge of a field. Go through a hedge gap, cross a track, go over a stile and head across a field to go through a kissing-gate in the middle bearing right before the field corner to a stile.

Climb the stile, cross a railway line, climb the stile opposite and continue gently downhill across a golf course. Cross a ditch, turn right, then turn left at a waymarked fingerpost to cross the second footbridge over the little River Brain and keep ahead to pick up a grassy path which continues gently uphill across the golf course to a stile by another fingerpost. After climbing it, keep ahead across a field and climb another stile on to a road at The Green Ⓑ. Turn right and almost immediately turn left, at a public footpath sign, on to a path that heads across a field, bearing slightly right to continue by a ditch on the right.

While the new golf course is under construction, follow the waymarkers heading for the buildings to Webb's Farm ahead and then turn left along a track and past a barrier on to Pole Lane. Turn right and take the first track on the left. The track winds between fields and, about 50 yds after passing a barn on the right, turn left at a waymarked post on to a concrete track, which later continues as a pleasant grassy track along the left-hand edge of fields. The track eventually becomes tree-lined and bends left to a fork. Take the right-hand track to emerge on to a road and turn right Ⓒ into White Notley, an attractive village with a fine medieval church. At a T-junction, turn left

The outstanding medieval timbered barns at Cressing Temple

along a lane, in the Silver End and Cressing direction, and cross a bridge over the River Brain .

At this point, those wishing to do the shorter walk should keep ahead along the lane.

For the full walk, immediately turn right – here joining the Essex Way – head across grass and continue along a track to a metal kissing-gate. Go through, walk along a straight, hedge-lined tarmac track, climb a stile and continue along the left-hand edge of a field. Climb another stile, walk along the left-hand edge of the next field and keep ahead, passing a footbridge over the River Brain, to a waymarked post. Turn left here and head gently uphill along the right-hand edge of a field, climb a stile and recross the railway line. Climb the stile opposite, keep

ahead to go through a kissing-gate and walk across the next field and through another kissing-gate to emerge on to a road opposite Cressing Temple. Climb the stile opposite, turn right along a fence-lined path and turn left to the entrance .

Cressing Temple originally belonged to the Knights Templars but after the order was suppressed by the Pope in 1308, it passed to the Knights Hospitallers. The present complex of buildings includes two of the finest medieval timbered barns in Europe, plus an Elizabethan Court Hall, early 17th-century farmhouse and an 18th-century Waggon Lodge. There is also a walled garden and moats. Since 1987 it has been owned by Essex County Council.

Retrace your steps to the lane by the

bridge over the river **D** and turn right to rejoin the shorter walk. At a public footpath sign, turn left along the enclosed, tarmac track to Fambridge Hall and turn left at a T-junction by the hall to continue along a gently descending track. Turn right along a track at an Essex Way post, pass under a railway bridge and the track winds across fields to a farm. Turn left here through a hedge gap, then continue along the field edge and turn right to a road. Cross the road to a public footpath sign, opposite **F** and continue along a path by a hedge on the right and continue in a straight line across fields to emerge on to a lane in front of Cressing's medieval church. The church has a Norman nave and 13th-century chancel.

Turn left into Cressing, keep ahead past the village green along The Street and, at a public footpath sign where the road forks **G**, turn left along an enclosed path beside a field. Keep ahead into the next field but immediately turn right over a plank footbridge and continue along the right-hand field edge. In the corner, turn right through a kissing-gate and turn left, continuing initially by the left-hand field edge but bearing right away from it to go through another kissing-gate.

Keep along the left-hand edge of the next two fields, by a ditch on the left. Follow the ditch around a left-hand bend and cross a footbridge over it. Turn right, continuing between a fence on the left and the ditch on the right, and the path turns first left and then right. After crossing a footbridge into trees, turn left along an enclosed path, bear left on joining a track and pass beside a gate on to a road on the edge of Tye Green.

Turn right, cross Mill Lane and, at a public footpath sign, turn left **H** along an enclosed, tarmac track. Pass beside a

vehicle scrapyard, keep ahead to climb a stile and continue across a field, making for a pylon where there is a waymarked post. Bear left to head across to the field corner, climb a stile, cross the railway line for the last time,

climb another stile and head downhill
along the left-hand field edge.

At the bottom, turn left along an
enclosed path, passing to the left of
Bulford Mill, climb a stile and keep
ahead to a lane. Turn left uphill and

follow the lane around right- and left-
hand bends to return to the starting
point at Cressing Station. .

SCALE 1:25000 or 2½ INCHES to 1 MILE 4CM to 1KM

Newport and Debden

Start

Newport Station.
Approx. 1 hour from
London Liverpool
Street

Distance

6½ miles (10.5km)

Height gain

330 feet (100m)

Approximate time

3 hours

Route terrain

Tracks, fields and
parkland paths, and
lanes

OS maps

Explorer 195 (Braintree
& Saffron Walden)

GPS waypoints

TL 522 335
Ⓐ TL 537 329
Ⓑ TL 552 323
Ⓒ TL 553 332
Ⓓ TL 545 338
Ⓔ TL 521 342

*By Essex standards this is a relatively hilly walk, rising to 345ft
on the first part of the route between Newport and Debden. The
return leg takes you across part of Debden Park and then on
through the valley of Debden Water. Both Newport and Debden
are attractive places with fine medieval churches.*

The long main street in Newport is lined by handsome buildings
dating from the late medieval period to the 19th century.
Foremost among these is the brick and timber-framed,
15th-century Monk's Barn. The 13th- to 15th-century church
has an imposing tower built in 1858.

Start by crossing the station footbridge, keep ahead
to a tarmac track and turn right. At a public
bridleway sign by the entrance to a huge
chalk quarry, turn left along a
pleasant, hedge - and tree-lined
path, which heads uphill to
emerge into a field. Keep
along the left-hand edge of
the field, following it as it
curves right, to a lane, turn
left and, where the lane
turns left, keep ahead Ⓐ
along the track to
Waldegraves Farm.

Continue along the track,
passing along the right-hand
edge of Cabbage Wood, and at
a fork take the right-hand
track to continue by the
edge of the wood. Look out
for where a waymarked post
directs you to turn first left
and then right and then head
gently downhill along the
right-hand edge of a field to reach
a lane by a picturesque, black and white
thatched cottage.

Turn left and, at a permissive footpath sign, turn left again  to walk along the right-hand edge of a field. Just before reaching the corner, turn right over a footbridge and turn left to keep along the left-hand edge of the next field, by woodland on the left. The path continues first along the right-hand, inside edge and later the left-hand, inside edge of the woodland, then becomes enclosed and bears left through a hedge gap. Turn right along the right-hand field edge, follow the edge to the left and continue up to a lane ⓒ. Turn right here for a short detour into the pretty village of Debden which has a pond, thatched cottages and a pub.

Retrace your steps along the lane and continue to the entrance to Debden churchyard. The church, which stands in a beautiful and isolated setting, dates mainly from the 13th century. Bear right along a waymarked path by the right-hand edge of the churchyard, and follow the path, which passes a kissing-gate to the churchyard and later crosses a bridge over a lake. Keep ahead along a track and, at a footpath sign, turn right to follow a path across Debden Park. To the right is a view of the lake.

At the far end of the field, keep ahead and walk along the left-hand edge of the next field and keep ahead to go through another kissing-gate on to a road. Turn right downhill, cross Debden Water and continue gently uphill to a public footpath sign ⓓ. Turn left here and, at a fork immediately ahead, take

SCALE 1:25000 or 2½ INCHES to 1 MILE 4CM to 1KM

0   200   400   600   800 METRES   1
                                   KILOMETRES
                                   MILES
0   200   400   600 YARDS   ½

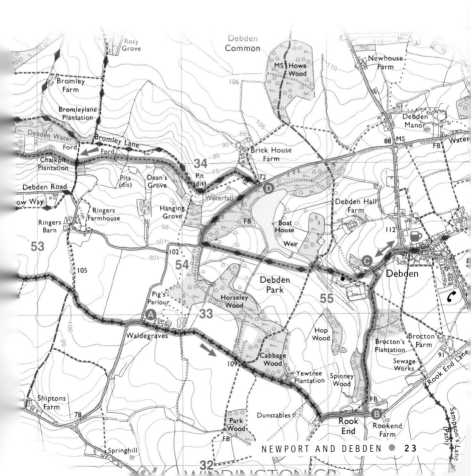

the left-hand track. Climb a stile, walk along a driveway, climb another stile and keep along the left-hand edge of the next field to go through a gate on the left. The path now curves along the right-hand field. Go over a stile. At a fork take the left-hand path, pass through a gap into the next field and curve left by the edge of woodland to continue across the middle of the field to a stile.

Climb it, keep ahead across a field, making for the corner of trees, and continue by the trees to a crossing of paths. Keep ahead beside conifers to the corner of the field and continue gently uphill along a broad, grassy ride between trees. As you keep along the winding right-hand edge of the next field, by trees on the right, the top of the tower of Newport church comes into view. In the field corner, keep ahead through a plantation, turn left to cross a footbridge over the infant River Cam and turn right to continue under a railway bridge.

Keep ahead along a tarmac track to the main street in Newport and turn left **E**. At the far end of the village, turn left again to return to the station. ●

A lane near Debden

Kent & East Sussex

The beach at Sandwich Bay

Kent & East Sussex

North Downs Way near Hollingbourne

Walking through the heart of Kent, it's hard to believe that this essentially rural corner of the country lies in the shadow of Docklands and the great glass towers of Canary Wharf. Known as Hellfire Corner during World War Two, Kent is one of those classic English counties with a distinctive identity and character. Added to that, the scenery is superb, with miles of desolate marshes, meandering river estuaries and remote secluded downland. This is where Charles Dickens sought solace and inspiration and Chaucer's Pilgrims journeyed to Canterbury.

At the heart of Kent lie the village of Wye and the dramatic landscape of the North Downs – ideal for discovering on foot. Away from signs of civilisation, this part of the county conveys a true sense of isolation and solitude – as if time has stood still. To the east are the villages of Hollingbourne and Thurnham and here also the area is dominated by spectacular ridges and fine views.

Farther west, at Shoreham, where South London's suburban sprawl gives way to the delights of the countryside, is a hidden corner of the county steeped in ancient history and tradition. No visit to Kent is complete, however, without a walk by the sea and the wonderfully varied 160-mile Saxon Shore Way at Sandwich Bay provides a fascinating glimpse of the county's famous and atmospheric coastline.

The Saxon Shore Way runs west into East Sussex and at picturesque Rye there is the chance to follow another popular trail, the Sussex Border Path, beside the meandering River Rother, or farther west, beyond Hastings, explore the Pevensey Levels by following in the footsteps of the Romans.

Inland is Battle, another historic site which draws countless tourists from all parts of the globe. Adjacent to the Abbey boundary miles of classic, gently undulating Sussex countryside stretch west to the Cuckmere River and Arlington Reservoir.

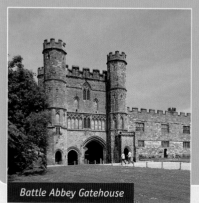
Battle Abbey Gatehouse

Hollingbourne and Thurnham

This route offers a fine physical challenge as well as the opportunity of enjoying one of the best sections of the North Downs Way, with the path constantly dipping and climbing. The views from the top of the ridge must be among the finest to be had from the North Downs Way.

walk 7

Start
Hollingbourne Station. Approx. 1 hour 10 minutes from London Victoria

Distance
9½ miles (15.2km)

Height gain
1,195 feet (365m)

Approximate time
4½ hours

Route terrain
Field and downland paths and tracks, and quiet lanes

OS maps
Explorer 148 (Maidstone and the Medway Towns)

GPS waypoints
  TQ 834 550
Ⓐ TQ 844 553
Ⓑ TQ 876 562
Ⓒ TQ 821 569
Ⓓ TQ 808 580
Ⓔ TQ 825 576
Ⓕ TQ 841 566

Walk along the leafy approach road from Hollingbourne Station and turn left at the T-junction with Eyhorne Street towards Hollingbourne. Continue under the railway bridge to pass the primary school (right) and, a little farther on, look for a war memorial on the left. Leave the road here for the tarmac path, left, and where this becomes a dirt path maintain direction across an arable field, heading for the corner of the churchyard. Follow the hedged path with the church on your right to emerge onto the church entrance lane. Walk out to Upper Street and turn left, following the road around to the right to reach a crossroads Ⓐ by the Dirty Habit pub; turn left. This quiet road is part of the ancient track known as the Pilgrims' Way. When the road reaches the hamlet of Broad Street, turn left after the Old House down a driveway, with an oast house to the right. The drive gives way to an enclosed path that ends when it reaches an open field. The right of way runs across farmland heading in a south-westerly direction.

Make for the left-hand corner of the woodland to the right Ⓑ, and you will come to a lone tree where five footpaths meet. A waymarker post stands by the tree. Turn sharp right and then follow the path with the wood to the left. Beyond the wood the path follows a ditch and reaches the drive leading to Ripple Manor. Turn right on to the drive that winds down to a cottage. Just before the cottage Ⓒ, at the beginning of a row of leylandii, turn left. A length of enclosed path follows and then a succession of stiles lead to paddocks. Keep ahead with fences to the left to reach steps that then take you towards the buildings of Cobham Manor Riding Centre.

From the car park, head for the road and turn left. Directly opposite the manor take a path on the right which heads across a field towards an oast house, where it meets a surfaced bridleway. Continue along this to reach Thurnham Lane and turn right to climb the hill, passing the Black Horse pub at the crossroads.

Keep straight on at the intersection and climb the steep hill to reach a hairpin bend where the North Downs Way leaves on the right . Take this path below the overgrown ramparts of Thurnham Castle, once a stronghold of the Norman family that gave the village its name. To the right is a steep combe that the path drops into and then climbs out of on the far side. This is the first of many similar exertions on this route. Turn right at the top of the combe to skirt the top of the field before descending steps below Civiley Wood. After these there is a much longer flight of steps to climb to reach the crest of the downs once again.

Some glorious walking follows along a grassy roller coaster of a path with a fine view to the right. More steps, up and down, follow through yew trees and fallen beeches. Shortly after the steps there are some fine beeches still standing which did well to survive the hurricane of 1987.

The path drops down to cross Coldblow Lane and a steep climb follows to the crest of the downs again near Cat's Mount. The North Downs Way now becomes an enfenced field-edge path with wide views to the south. It then descends again to cross the neck of a large field and then meets a byway . This is Coldharbour Lane; turn left and follow it up to reach the top of the ridge once again. Here the North Downs Way leaves to the right. Follow it as it wends its way through woodland just below the crest as before, with glimpses of great, mile-long fields below.

The path emerges from woodland and then crosses a large field. After this it crosses another field above Broad Street, with the boundary close by on the right, before reaching another road. Cross over to resume walking along the ridge on a grassy path. A further flight of steps in a wood takes the path down to the byway that climbs up from Allington Farm. Turn left for a short way up this muddy track and then turn off right on to a winding path that passes through

Looking east along the North Downs near Hollingbourne

Hucking Estate woodland.

For a short distance the path meanders through the trees and then the woodland suddenly ends and a wide view over the Weald is revealed. Another short stretch of woodland follows before the path reaches open hillside again. Continue to follow the North Downs Way signs, bearing right towards Hollingbourne when you approach a line of yew trees and the church and village can be seen below. A lone post serves as a waymark on the downland slope here, though it is hard to miss the way with the road ahead. The path does not join the road immediately, however, but runs parallel to and above it. It then descends gradually to meet the road on the edge of Hollingbourne **(A)**. Retrace your outward route to Hollingbourne Station.

SCALE 1:27777 or 2¼ INCHES to 1 MILE 3.6CM to 1KM

| 0 | 200 | 400 | 600 | 800 METRES | 1 |
| 0 | 200 | 400 | 600 YARDS | ½ | KILOMETRES MILES |

walk 8

Start

Shoreham Station.
Approx. 45 minutes
from London Victoria
Approx. 50 minutes
from London
Blackfriars

Distance

7¾ miles (12.4km)

Height gain

900 feet (275m)

Approximate time

3½ hours

Route terrain

Downland, woodland
and parkland tracks
and paths

OS maps

Explorers 147
(Sevenoaks &
Tonbridge) and 162
(Greenwich &
Gravesend)

GPS waypoints

　　TQ 526 615
Ⓐ TQ 512 630
Ⓑ TQ 509 639
Ⓒ TQ 506 646
Ⓓ TQ 521 654
Ⓔ TQ 523 633

Shoreham and Lullingstone Park

This pleasant walk combines rolling Kent downland with the Darent Valley Path. The outward part of the route climbs to the top of the downs and covers woodland, fields and parkland, and the return follows the lovely valley of the River Darent, passing Lullingstone Roman Villa and the World Garden of Plants at Lullingstone Castle. There are a few short uphill sections but none are more severe than the climb at the start from Shoreham to the top of Meenfield Wood.

Walk down to the main road and turn sharp right into Station Road to pass under the railway bridge and stride out towards Shoreham. *Care is required as there is no pavement but make use of the verge when this is available.* Bend right and then left with the lane by Ye Olde George Inn and keep ahead on Church Street, crossing the River Darent to reach a T-junction. Turn right into High Street and after about 100 yds turn left into The Landway towards Timberden Bottom. This is a steep path which strikes directly up the hill and crosses the track at the edge of Meenfield Wood. Continue climbing into the wood, cross the track at the top, and drop down towards Timberden Farm. When the path emerges at a stile, head for the lovely house with the white fence below. Cross two fields, and turn right over the stile onto Shacklands Road.

Carry straight on at the road junction but 100 yds after this

View across the Darent Valley

turn left on to Cockerhurst Road. This becomes quite steep and when it veers

left leave it to the right opposite a bungalow. This footpath continues to climb beside a hawthorn thicket on the right, with fine views if you look back. Near the top of the hill bear right over a

0	200	400	600	800 METRES	1
					KILOMETRES
					MILES
0	200	400	600 YARDS	½

stile  and follow a wire fence along the eastern perimeter of Dalhanna. Keep the spinney, and then a hedge, to the left as the path heads for a modern cottage near the electricity lines ahead. Bear left at the cottage and join a concrete track which leads to a road.

Turn left here and after a short distance, at the end of the field to the right, look for steps up the bank on the right. Take the field path to pass to the left of sheds of corrugated iron on the right and reach a metal gate **B** into Upper Beechen Wood. The right of way crosses straight over a footpath junction and then there is a short stretch through pleasant woodland. The path unexpectedly emerges from this on to a golf course fairway. Cross the fairway to find another small tract of woodland which gives way to a wider expanse of golf course. Follow the waymarks past the clubhouse and enter the car park.

The hillside cross at Shoreham

Walk across to the exit gate and bear right onto the track **C** towards Holmesdale Hall.

Pass the large black barns and modern bungalows on your right, then settle into your stride for a long stretch of straight field-edge track and path, with poplar trees along the edge. Cross a stile, then go through a footpath gate so the poplars are on the right.

Before Hulberry the path bears left. Go through the small gate **D** on your right, and follow the waymarked path around to the right. Halfway down the hill, zigzag through the hedge on your left. Here are good views of Eynsford, with its splendid red brick viaduct, as the path drops to the drive leading to Lullingstone Castle. Turn right when the path meets the drive, close to the site of Lullingstone's famous Roman villa, joining the Darent Valley Path. The river is to the left as the drive leads to the castle. The gatehouse is all that remains of the original castle – the present house is an imposing Queen Anne mansion.

This part of the route is popular with visitors to Lullingstone Park, and the path by the lake and then by the river is likely to be busy on fine days. It is a very pretty footpath which ends at the visitors' centre at the south end of the lake.

Just beyond the car park entrance, cross the stile into a field and follow the footpath parallel to the road. Continue past the 'Hop Shop' as far as the corner of the field **E**. Drop down the steps on your left, cross the road, and rejoin the Darent Valley Path as it strikes across fields to reach the riverside again. At Mill House the path turns left and then right before continuing by the River Darent to Shoreham. At the attractive old bridge turn left into Church Street and keep ahead to follow Station Road back to the start.

Pevensey Levels

Start
Pevensey & Westham
Station. Approx. 1
hour 40 minutes from
London Victoria

Distance
5½ miles (8.8km)

Height gain
Negligible

Approximate time
2½ hours

Route terrain
Field and riverside
paths

OS maps
Explorers 123
(Eastbourne & Beachy
Head) and 124
(Hastings & Bexhill)

GPS waypoints
TQ 638 043
Ⓐ TQ 638 047
Ⓑ TQ 639 058
Ⓒ TQ 626 068
Ⓓ TQ 630 067
Ⓔ TQ 637 063
Ⓕ TQ 642 054

The meadowlands of the Pevensey Levels may be flat but they are seldom tedious, especially to the naturalist or ornithologist. These pastures are lonely and the landscape is dominated by the mood of the sky. This route explores footpaths and bridleways that lead through countryside largely neglected by walkers, and it is interesting to speculate on how the landscape appeared some 2,000 years ago when the Romans made Pevensey a fortified gateway into Britain. One thousand years later Saxon outlaws probably used the marshlands to escape from the Norman overlords. Follow the route directions carefully: the meadows are grazed by cows and heifers, occasionally accompanied by a bull.

Leave Pevensey and Westham Station to turn right onto the main road, B2191 Eastbourne Road, and right again at the roundabout to walk along High Street. After 200 yds turn left into Peelings Lane, passing the village hall. Bear right when the road forks by the end of the pond. Turn right again at Castle Farm Ⓐ, where a small notice announces 'Alsation loose', climb a stile leading out of the farmyard, and head straight on over the brow of the low rise in the meadow ahead towards the bypass. Climb a stile and keep ahead, crossing a footbridge and another stile to reach the road.

After crossing carefully, climb a stile and head directly across the meadow towards an observatory seen on the horizon – the route is well-waymarked – going through a gate and over a stile to reach a footbridge and waymarked post Ⓑ. At the post, do not cross the bridge but take the bridleway left along the south bank of Pevensey Haven. It is little use looking for breakwaters and quays here, since the river has long been closed for navigation. Instead, you may see herons or kingfishers hunting its peaceful waters.

The bridleway continues, close by the bank of the placid waterway, until a tall pylon ahead heralds the end of this pleasant section. The path skirts the left side of the farmyard at Bridge Farm to reach a quiet country lane Ⓒ. Turn right and then immediately right again onto the road to Pevensey that crosses the river, which is now known as the Yotham. Continue down the road for nearly ¼ mile, passing beneath electricity cables and following the road as it bends left at a gate giving access to an angling club, and then left again. At this second corner Ⓓ cross a stile on the right at a

The remains of the Norman castle of Pevensey

footpath sign.

From here the tower of Pevensey church can be seen to the south east and this landmark is a useful guide on the next section of the walk, over water meadows to Chilley Green.

After crossing the stile walk a few paces to the left, climb another stile and bear left around the edge of the meadow. There is a stile and footbridge by a clump of bushes on the far side. After crossing the bridge turn right to walk along the field edge beside a ditch. This will eventually bring you to a gate. Pass through this to another gate ahead, then keep left beside the hedge and follow a short track to the road at Chilley Green Ⓔ. Turn right and

then right again, immediately after the farm, onto a track which leads to Chilley Farm Shop. Pass in front of the shop and beside a pond, then go through a gate on the left just beyond the farmyard. Cross the field to a footbridge and continue directly across the next two fields, heading once more for the tower of Pevensey church.

This leads to the banks of Pevensey Haven again and to a long footbridge. Cross the bridge Ⓑ and turn left, following the bridleway along the waterside until a blue waymark on a post Ⓕ directs you to a metal gate, from where a path leads, with a couple of twists, to the bypass. Cross carefully again, go through

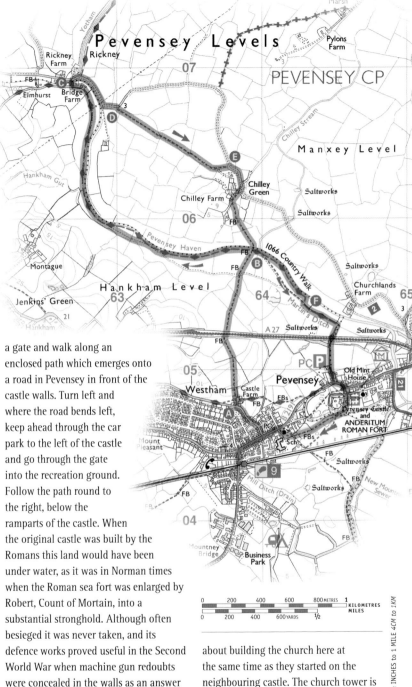

a gate and walk along an enclosed path which emerges onto a road in Pevensey in front of the castle walls. Turn left and where the road bends left, keep ahead through the car park to the left of the castle and go through the gate into the recreation ground. Follow the path round to the right, below the ramparts of the castle. When the original castle was built by the Romans this land would have been under water, as it was in Norman times when the Roman sea fort was enlarged by Robert, Count of Mortain, into a substantial stronghold. Although often besieged it was never taken, and its defence works proved useful in the Second World War when machine gun redoubts were concealed in the walls as an answer to the threat of German invasion.

The sea once lapped against the walls of the eastern and southern perimeter of the castle, and the footpath skirts these by pretty meadows to reach the churchyard of St Mary's, Westham. The Normans set

about building the church here at the same time as they started on the neighbouring castle. The church tower is squat yet powerful, a symbol of strength which, though not tall, is a distinctive landmark.

Turn left out of the churchyard onto the main road and follow it back to the railway station.

SCALE 1:25000 or 2½ INCHES to 1 MILE 4CM to 1KM

walk 10

Start

Battle Station. Approx.
1 hour 30 minutes
from London Charing
Cross

Distance

5¼ miles (8.4km)

Height gain

655 feet (200m)

Approximate time

2½ hours

Route terrain

Field and woodland
paths and lanes

OS maps

Explorer 124 (Hastings
& Bexhill)

GPS waypoints

  TQ 754 155
Ⓐ TQ 746 160
Ⓑ TQ 742 154
Ⓒ TQ 737 149
Ⓓ TQ 741 135
Ⓔ TQ 745 134
Ⓕ TQ 743 144
Ⓖ TQ 744 147

Around Battle

This undulating walk has great historic interest as it traverses part of the site of what is generally regarded as the most significant battle in English history and there are views of the battlefield and of Battle Abbey from various points.

Bear left on leaving Battle Station, walking along Station Approach to the T-junction and turning right. Stay with the main road, A2100, rising into the town, swinging left by The Chequers and passing St Mary the Virgin Church. Pass Mount Street (right) and immediately before the Almonry, turn left down the narrow Western Avenue Ⓐ. Pass Woodhams Close, zigzag right and left at the bottom, then go through the kissing-gate onto a country path.

Continue through a few trees before bearing left along the side of a long, narrow field. Keep well to the left as the path drops over a stile into the corner of Saxon Wood. Follow it over a brook, then up a few steps and over a stile; now keep ahead, before turning right and bending left with the track to a junction.

Fork right at the fingerpost towards Pevensey Ⓑ, and follow the waymarked 1066 Country Walk as it bears right and drops into the woods. Continue until the track leaves the woods through a second gate; almost at once turn left over the stile Ⓒ, cross a large field, and enter Warren Wood at a stile.

Keep ahead along the woodland path as it winds right, then left, keeping the railings at Farthing Pond on your right. Then bear right over the footbridge, and keep ahead along the

The site of the Battle of Hastings

waymarked 'Short Walk' that runs up a concrete track and continues to the gate at Powdermill Lane. Cross and follow the waymarked road towards Millers Farm, bear left past Miller's Oast, then keep ahead through the gates to a signpost at the corner of a barn. Turn right to walk beside the farm buildings, cross two stiles, then turn left onto the waymarked track that drops to gates in the shallow valley **D**.

Turn left along an enclosed track, then continue along the side of an open field towards a large electricity pylon. A waymarked stile leads along a narrow enclosed path beneath the pylon and out onto a track. Keep ahead to the crossways at Powdermill Cottage **E**.

Turn left onto the surfaced lane, cross the bridge and continue past Peppering Eye Farm to the junction with Telham Lane. Turn left to meet Powdermill Lane.

Cross the road, nip over the stile **F**, and bear right onto the 1066 Bexhill Walk. Follow the trees on your right to an access road with a stile on each side **G**.

Cross both stiles and bear right along the gravel track beside the trees. Go through a wicket gate and a narrow belt of trees, then keep ahead, climbing gently beside the hedge and continuing through two gates to a sturdy fingerpost near the brow of the hill **B**.

Bear right towards Battle and follow the well-made path beside the woodland fence until it emerges through a wicket gate and brings you to the Abbey gatehouse. Turn right and reverse your outward route to complete the walk. ●

SCALE 1:25 000 or 2½ INCHES to 1 MILE 4CM to 1KM

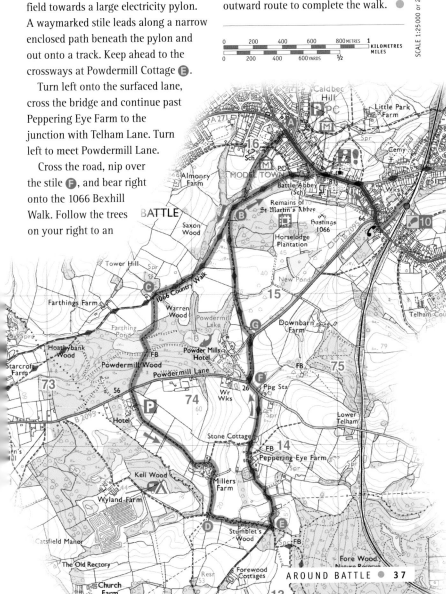

walk 11

Sandwich and Sandwich Bay

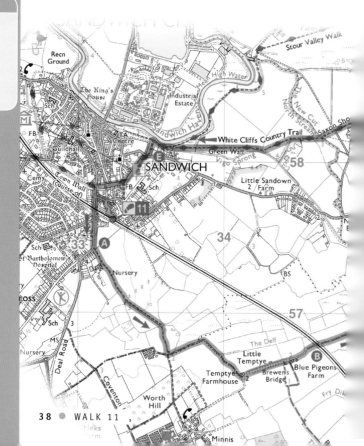

Start

Sandwich Station.
Approx. 1 hour 50
minutes from London
St Pancras

Distance

5½ miles (8.8km)

Height gain

Negligible

Approximate time

2½ hours

Route terrain

Undemanding field
paths and lanes

OS maps

Explorer 150
(Canterbury and the
Isle of Thanet)

GPS waypoints

TR 332 576
Ⓐ TR 331 574
Ⓑ TR 346 568
Ⓒ TR 355 575
Ⓓ TR 362 579
Ⓔ TR 335 581

Sandwich is an historic former port and this easy walk follows paths across drained farmland to the wide, pebble beach at Sandwich Bay before returning across a golf course and passing by Sandwich Haven on the River Stour.

Head away from the station along Delfside to turn left at the T-junction into St Georges Road and, in about 100 yds, left again into New Street. Follow the road over the level-crossing, past St Bartholomew's Chapel and where the road bends to the right Ⓐ take the asphalt footpath on the left. Follow it as it veers left away from the drainage dyke. Eventually, cross the dyke by the footbridge and turn left by the white house onto an asphalted bridleway. The track curves right towards Temptye Farmhouse. Over to the right is the spire of the church in Worth village. Turn left at the farmhouse, taking the track past Little Temptye. Carry on straight ahead at Blue Pigeons Farm, ignoring the bridleway to the right, to cross the railway line Ⓑ.

Follow the path to Little Downs Bridge across North Stream, passing by the curve of the stream to pick up a track by a second curve in the river. Follow the track, ignoring a footpath to left and right, to pass the Sandwich Bay Bird Observatory to Guilford Road  .

Go straight across the road to the stile into the field and cross to the corner. Follow cement footpath markers to enter the golf course. Follow the mown path across the course, watching for more cement footpath markers. Leave the golf course, cross Princes Drive to the beach **D**. This is Sandwich Bay. To the north is Pegwell Bay, where St Augustine landed to

Sandwich Bay

bring Christianity to England in 597. The Saxons also landed here. The town beyond is Ramsgate.

Turn left along the shore. The best walking is between the beach and the road, on the grassy path. Turn left by the public toilet block to take the stile back onto the golf course. Follow the well-marked paths across a fairway, past the clubhouse to a kissing gate. Cross an asphalt track to a stile leading to a footbridge. Pick up the asphalt path, continuing easily for a little more than ½ mile to cross a footbridge over a tributary of the Stour, then turning right to follow the bank of the main river towards a children's playground **E**. Turn left following signs for the Saxon Shore Way. Pass the tennis club, turn right at the road to cross the bridge then turn left along the line of the old town wall. Ignore the path going left down steps but follow the curve of the old wall, passing allotments and bowling greens. Turn left at New Street, leaving the Saxon Shore Way and then first left into St Georges Road. Reverse your outward route back to the railway station.

SCALE 1:25000 or 2½ INCHES to 1 MILE 4CM to 1KM

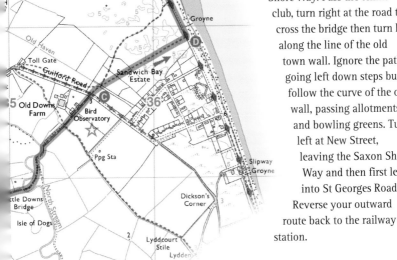

Iden from Rye

Start

Rye Station. Approx. 1 hour 15 minutes from London St Pancras

Distance

6 miles (9.7km)

Height gain

310 feet (95m)

Approximate time

3 hours

Route terrain

Town centre roads, field and riverside paths

OS maps

Explorer 125 (Romney Marsh, Rye & Winchelsea)

GPS waypoints

TQ 919 205
Ⓐ TQ 925 206
Ⓑ TQ 932 225
Ⓒ TQ 925 235
Ⓓ TQ 914 232
Ⓔ TQ 911 219
Ⓕ TQ 912 215
Ⓖ TQ 916 208

Parking at Rye is at a premium in the summer but taking the train presents a way of overcoming the problem. Although some of the paths on the route seem to be underused, it gives unusual views of the town and the freedom to take time to explore it fully. At times careful map-reading is needed.

Standing with your back to the station walk ahead along the main road (A268). Follow it left through Rye town centre to turn right up East Cliff, under the archway, then left for a few paces down a sloping path. At the bottom, cross at the pedestrian crossing, turn left passing in front of a car park and take the A259 right, keeping ahead to cross the River Rother and then turn left to join the Saxon Shore Way Ⓐ.

The path forms part of the Saxon Shore Way, the Sussex Border Path and the Royal Military Canal footpath. There is little headroom as it goes beneath the railway bridge but after this the walking is enjoyable, with the river and gentle hills to the left and Romney Marsh to the right. Cross the Union Canal and, ½ mile farther on, turn left to cross the river at Scots Float Sluice Ⓑ.

Cross the road to a footbridge on the other side, which forms the start of a path that climbs into a wood, with steps helping the ascent up steep slopes. The stile at the top gives on to a clearly defined path across a large field. Cross the next field diagonally to Houghton Wood. The path goes through the wood, a stream using it in wet weather. After the second of two plank bridges the right of way leaves the trees, crosses the neck of a field and then follows the field edge towards a farmhouse (curiously known as Old Turks).

Go right at the road, then left across a stile onto a waymarked footpath opposite Old Turks Ⓒ. Cross the field diagonally to a stile on the left of a metal gate. Keep ahead with a pond to the right, and then follow the boundary hedge, avoiding a waymarked path on the right. Keep to the field edge, then just before reaching a gateway, bear right through a gap in the hedge to follow a path (not waymarked) across the centre of a field to a stile. Continue across the next field to a stile and a narrow path leading to a road. Turn left to a crossroads by the

Bell and cross over into Church Lane, following it to All Saints' Church.

Iden wins a mention in *The Guinness Book of Records* as the two rectors who held office from 1807 served 117 years between them, the second one dying in 1924. The sturdy, battlemented tower is the main feature of the church, dating from the 11th century.

Walk past the west end of the church to a group of small oak trees in the

The approach to Rye

corner of the playing field. Here a well-concealed and unwaymarked footpath starts on the left, swinging right to reach a stile. After this it follows the edge of a field with a fence to the left, descending to a plank bridge and stile at the bottom. Follow the waymark to the right and make your way through a 'conservation meadow', planted with uniform lines of fruit trees. Beyond them cross a field, go through a gate and keep left along the field edge to a stile by an asbestos hut.

Cross a bridleway and the stile on the other side ⓓ and keep ahead to find a metal stile by a beech tree. Turn right to follow a hedge down to the corner of Tighe's Wood. The path is faint as it leads along the edge of the wood and descends to another metal stile at the end of a row of sweet chestnut trees. The path is more obvious as it climbs with a fence to the left to a stile and continue to reach the A268, meeting the road at a weatherboarded cottage.

Turn left for 20 yds and then go right on a grassy bridleway, dropping down into a little valley. Make for the field corner and continue on the path when it becomes enclosed by trees and bushes.

Pass a path on the left and soon follow the path right into a field, keeping right into an adjacent field corner ⓔ. Turn left along the field edge until you see a waymark and swing right across the field, heading uphill towards the boundary.

The steady climb leads you to a gap in the hedge close to the field corner. Keep ahead along a field edge path to a stile and enter the yard of Leasam Farm. Keep ahead past Leasam Byre and, where the drive swings left, leave it to the right ⓕ to follow a fenced path through woodland. Cross an asphalted driveway to a kissing-gate that gives the first view of Rye with its windmill well seen ahead. There is an even better view from the stile a little way farther down Leasam Hill, at the top of a belt of trees.

Descend to Rolvendene Farm, go through a gate and bear left in front of the farm, then keep right to follow the path along the grassy embankment between the river and the drive. Go right when you reach a surfaced footpath ⓖ and pass a row of terrace houses before coming to the main road. Turn left to the level-crossing and first left back to Rye Station. ●

Wye and Crundale Downs

A section of this walk which uses the North Downs Way has some spectacular long-distance views. Elsewhere on the route there are many other, more intimate views of the Kent countryside, which give just as much pleasure. The outward leg uses part of the Stour Valley Walk and the long section which follows heading south is on a quiet byway and footpath along the crest of the Crundale Downs.

Start
Wye Station. Approx. 1 hour from London St Pancras

Distance
9½ miles (15.2km)

Height gain
1,065 feet (325m)

Approximate time
4½ hours

Route terrain
Downland and woodland tracks and paths; undulating route with two steep climbs and one steep descent

OS maps
Explorer 137 (Ashford)

GPS waypoints
TR 048 469
Ⓐ TR 062 469
Ⓑ TR 067 473
Ⓒ TR 075 477
Ⓓ TR 076 488
Ⓔ TR 084 485
Ⓕ TR 087 468
Ⓖ TR 082 462
Ⓗ TR 086 448
Ⓙ TR 077 457
Ⓚ TR 070 469

Wye's fame lies in its agricultural college, a part of the University of London, but few people realise that the college is based upon a medieval foundation, some of which can still be seen at the eastern side of the churchyard. The ancient buildings were erected by John Kempe, Archbishop of Canterbury, who in 1432 founded a college which was originally used to train priests. After the Dissolution it was a grammar school, and in the early years of the 20th century became an agricultural college.

 Leave the station and turn left along Bridge Street, soon crossing the pretty River Stour. After the Tickled Trout pub turn left and follow Churchfield Way through Wye all the way to the Church of St Gregory & St Martin. Follow the Stour Valley Walk waymark through the churchyard to the north-eastern corner, on to a footpath which passes allotments. Turn right at a road, go past college buildings and cross another, more major, road on to Occupation Road, which is waymarked with a North Downs Way logo.

Occupation Road passes offices, sheds and nurseries belonging to the agricultural college and heads east in a straight line towards the escarpment of the downs. Beyond the buildings the fields are sheltered by various windbreaks – conifers, poplars and hawthorns – and just before the end of these leave the track by turning left on to a path Ⓐ across fields, following the Stour Valley Way emblem.

After a spinney, with stiles at either end, cross a road to a track on the opposite side which leads up through young trees to a radio mast. Follow the path which leaves the track to the left before the mast and goes through a planting of beeches before crossing another lane. Emerging from the wood turn

The view from Crundale church

right **B** on to a good field track. There is a fine view to the north from here. At the end of the wood follow a path which soon strikes across the field, rising steeply as it nears narrow Beech Wood on the far side.

The climb continues through the wood and up to the top of the meadow on the other side – the summit of Marriage Hill. The name derives from the ancient *moere hyreg*, meaning a boundary ridge.

The way dips down into a hollow, then rises to cross a stile beside a gate to reach a junction of five paths **C**. Turn left along the Stour Valley Walk, the path following the edge of Warren Wood with a fence to the right. At the end of the field is a stile into the wood and the path soon joins a grassy track with a fence to the left. Easy walking soon ends, however, as the track becomes rutted and muddy as it drops down steeply to leave the wood. There is then a good field path leading north towards Crundale village, and this meets a track **D** at the top end of Warren Wood.

Turn right to walk past the northern end of Marriage Wood on a lovely green lane which later becomes much more of a farm track. Crundale church can be seen on top of the hill ahead. Descend

to the second white house, pass to the right of it and follow the track as it climbs up the flank of the hill, but before the top turn right on to another

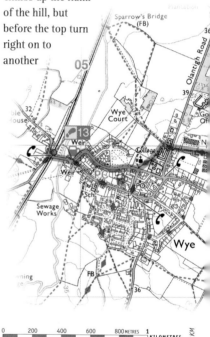

SCALE 1:25 000 or 2½ INCHES to 1 MILE 4CM to 1KM

bridleway and then almost immediately left over a stile by a gate to the left **E**. Climb to the top of the paddock to a stile opposite the east end of the church – a remote building which dates from early Norman times – and turn right on to a good track which strikes south along the top of the downs, with an old steeplechase course to the right at first.

Crundale Downs, though no longer an open sheepwalk, are nevertheless still splendid. Their attraction is mainly due to their isolation but it is exhilarating walking here with larks singing above and ever-changing views over an expanse of countryside. Almost too soon you

chippings have been laid to aid progress. It drops down to meet a lane to Hassell Street.

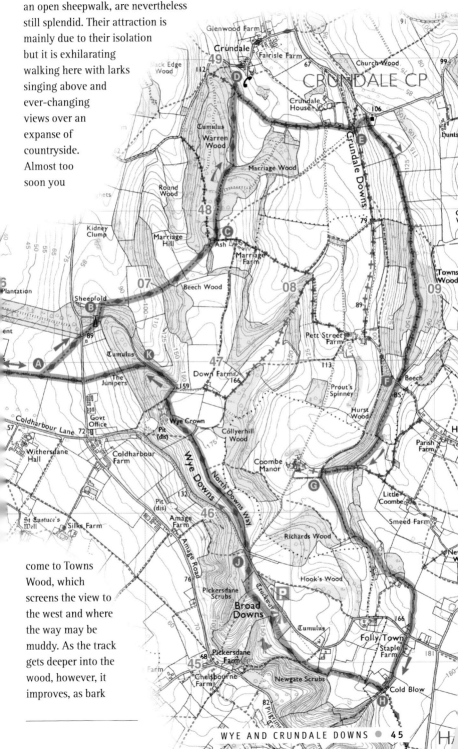

come to Towns Wood, which screens the view to the west and where the way may be muddy. As the track gets deeper into the wood, however, it improves, as bark

View from Crundale Downs

Cross the lane **F** to a path which follows the right-hand edge of two fields on a generous headland. At the end of the second field go through a gate and descend into the crater to find a stile on the other side. Then follow the grassy track – its ancient course is etched into the chalk – to the bottom of the field **G** and turn left to follow the fence away from Coombe Manor.

The path climbs up to the woods again to a stile at the end of the field. Pass through a gate and beyond this keep to the right-hand side of a paddock to a stile at the end. Cross the next field diagonally to a stile at the top corner. The stile after this takes the footpath on to the driveway from Stoackes Cottage. Turn left and follow the drive to the road at Folly Town.

Cross over the road and walk past Staple Farm and the farmyard at Cold Blow. Turn right over a stile, before the National Nature Reserve's noticeboard, on to the North Downs Way **H**. The path goes across the field to a field-edge path which skirts the top of Newgate Scrubs to reach open downland. This is a celebrated part of the North Downs Way, with unmatched views to the west over Brook and Wye to Ashford and the Wealden countryside beyond. The road is close to the right and to the left is the Devil's Kneading Trough, a spectacular steep-sided combe. The restaurant which bears the same name is on the other side of the road to the right.

The walking within the nature reserve is on turf which is kept in 'unimproved condition' – that is as it would have been on downland before intensive agriculture supplanted the traditional sheepwalk. Rare plants, including orchids like the Maid of Kent or lady orchid, are protected here. After leaving the reserve the North Downs Way crosses the road **J** just to the north-west of the restaurant.

There is a byway immediately opposite the point at which the North Downs Way meets the road, and the long-distance route continues through the gate to the left of this. Keep the fence to the right as Wye comes into view ahead. Continue over the high ground, passing a memorial stone to a man who loved walking the downs. A milepost indicates Farnham is 101 miles from here, Canterbury and Dover both 21. At the end of the long field climb over a stile and continue following the fence to a stile on the right when the way ahead is blocked. The path skirts round the top of a small piece of woodland to reach the road. Turn left and walk along the road with a pleasant valley to the right. Leave the road to the left **K** just before it swings to the right, following the North Downs Way sign on to a bridleway through a wood, then along the edge of a field and across a road before rejoining the outward route at **A**, near the college of agriculture. Retrace your outward steps to return to Wye Station. ●

Arlington and Abbot's Wood

An easy, level walk that follows the Wealdway across farmland, close to the Cuckmere River, to Michelham Priory, a beautiful moated historic house, before returning through Abbot's Wood to Arlington village. Allow time to visit the interesting flint Church of St Pancras and enjoy a spot of bird watching from the hide beside Arlington Reservoir.

Start
Berwick Station
Approx. 1 hour 30 minutes from London Victoria

Distance
9½ miles (15.2km)

Height gain
375 feet (115m)

Approximate time
4½ hours

Route terrain
Field and woodland paths

OS maps
Explorer 123 (Eastbourne & Beachy Head)

GPS waypoints
- TQ 526 067
- Ⓐ TQ 543 081
- Ⓑ TQ 552 099
- Ⓒ TQ 561 094
- Ⓓ TQ 566 091
- Ⓔ TQ 562 084
- Ⓕ TQ 557 072
- Ⓖ TQ 543 074

Completed in 1971 to supply 23 million litres of water daily to the Eastbourne and Hailsham areas, Arlington Reservoir is also an important local nature reserve, a favoured haunt for many migrant birds, including the Osprey, and a wintering ground for up to 10,000 wildfowl.

 Leave the tiny Berwick Station and turn left by the level-crossing into Station Road, keeping ahead for ½ mile to reach a car park entrance (right) signed to Arlington Reservoir. Cross the grassy area in front of the car park and bear left to follow the lower path beside the reservoir. Keep ahead where the path merges with a bridleway and soon reach a fork of paths by an information board. Follow the fence ahead to a gate and keep to the left-hand field edge, passing beneath power cables. Follow the field edge right and soon pass in front of Sessingham Farm to cross a driveway and footbridge. Follow the bridleway right to reach a bridge Ⓐ over the Cuckmere River.

Climb the stile just before the bridge to join the Wealdway and walk parallel with the river. Go though a gate, continue along the right-hand field edge, soon to bear half-left across the open field, keeping right of the telegraph pole and oak trees to locate a footbridge on the field edge. Cross the footbridge, bear left to a stile and walk across two fields to reach a stile to the right of a brick cottage. Turn left along the tarmac drive, then almost immediately cross the stile on the right and walk beside the woodland to a stile in the field corner. Keep ahead along the edge of the golf course, cross a stile by a noticeboard and then the stile ahead to follow a hedged path right to reach the road. Turn right into Upper Dicker, passing The Plough and St Bede's School before following the Wealdway right just before the village shop Ⓑ.

Pass between houses to a stile, cross a paddock and a further stile and plank bridge, then bear slightly right across a playing

View towards Arlington church

through a clearing on the edge of Wilmington Wood. As it widens, keep left of the wires to locate a bridleway that descends into the wood to cross a footbridge. Look out for a green barrier **E** on the left and follow the forest track beyond it into Abbot's Wood, a mixed woodland of approximately 360 hectares that derives its name from the times of Henry I, when the wood was gifted to Battle Abbey and overseen by the Abbot (hence Abbot's Wood).

Keep ahead at a crossing towards 'The Lake' and remain on the main path as it skirts the lake and curves right through the wood. Continue ahead on merging with a track, do the same at the next junction and descend to a crossing of paths. Follow the narrower path ahead to reach the car park **F**.

Exit the wood via the tarmac access road and turn left to reach a road junction. Take the footpath over a stile on the right beyond the post box. Cross the stiles and drive to your left and turn

field to another stile. Keep left along the field edge, cross a stile and turn left to follow a diagonal path to the far end of farm buildings and a track. Turn left over the bridge at the edge of England's longest water-filled medieval moat, which surrounds Michelham Priory (hidden in trees). The Priory was founded in 1229 for 12 canons and a prior and includes the remains of the former Augustinian priory (open), a Tudor mansion filled with furniture and artefacts, a 14th-century gatehouse, a medieval watermill, and a dramatic Elizabethan Great Barn. Continue to cross a second bridge and follow the Wealdway right through a narrow field to a gate **C**.

Leave the Wealdway, bearing half-left to a stile on the edge of Bramble Grove. Follow the path through the wood to a gate and turn right around the field edge to a stile. Follow the wide byway right and head uphill beside woodland. At the top of the rise **D** bear left downhill to reach a road.

Turn left, then in 100 yds take the arrowed path sharp right and follow the line of telegraph poles right along the field edge to a stile. Keep ahead, soon to bear left around the field edge to reach a stile in a hedge on your right. Go straight across the field ahead to double stiles, then fork left to a stile and road. Turn right into Arlington, bearing right at the Yew Tree Inn to the church **G**.

Walk through the churchyard, bear left to a gate and follow the path ahead to cross a stile. Turn right, cross the footbridge over the Cuckmere River and head uphill to the reservoir. Pass through the gate (bird hide signed right) and turn left along the reservoir wall to a track. Turn right, skirt around Polhill's Farm on a fenced path, then cross the track to follow the grassy path close to the reservoir back to the car park. Exit this and turn left to return to Berwick Station.

SCALE 1:25000 or 2½ INCHES to 1 MILE 4CM to 1KM

15 Arundel Park and the River Arun

Pavement and parkland, woodland and riverside paths

4¼ miles (6.8km)

2 hours

16 Fishbourne and Bosham

Flat tracks and field paths

5¼ miles (8.4km)

2½ hours

17 The Wey and Arun Canal from Billingshurst

Field and canalside paths

6¾ miles (10.8km)

3 hours

18 Limpsfield

Pavement and undulating woodland paths

8½ miles (13.6km)

4 hours

19 Witley to Haslemere via Chiddingfold

Lanes, woodland and grassy paths

7¼ miles (11.6km)

3½ hours

20 Gomshall to the Abingers

Woodland paths and enclosed tracks, some quiet country lanes

8 miles (13km)

4 hours

21 Box Hill

Lanes, tracks and woodland paths

11¾ miles (18.8km)

6 hours

The weir at Walsham Lock, Surrey

Surrey & West Sussex

Woodland at Gomshall

Generally regarded as sprawling commuterland and bisected by busy roads and congested motorways, the real Surrey and West Sussex could not be more different. Away from the noise and bustle, leafy Surrey, only 20 miles from the centre of London, is characterised by a spectacular rolling landscape that includes some of the best viewpoints in the south of England.

From a walker's perspective, Surrey has everything – wooded hills, undulating downland, pretty river valleys and sandstone escarpments. One of the county's best-known natural landmarks is Box Hill, named after the ancient box trees on its flanks. With its impressive scenery and numerous branch paths and tracks, the North Downs Way offers the perfect opportunity to get to know Surrey on foot. Running roughly west to east through the heart of the county, the trail connects many much-loved beauty spots and picturesque villages, including Box Hill, Gomshall and Limpsfield, which lies close to Surrey's border with Kent.

The countryside where Surrey meets West Sussex is no less attractive. The historic town of Haslemere and the charming village of Chiddingfold lie at the heart of some classic walking country. Delightfully rural West Sussex is the perfect walker's playground. Situated on the edge of the newly designated South Downs National Park is the commuter village of Billingshurst, a good starting point for numerous level easy walks, while to the south lie magnificent Arundel Park and its magical castle, bisected by some very pleasant paths and trails. The more demanding long-distance Monarch's Way also crosses this fine parkland landscape. To the west a maze of breezy coastal walks can be found around the villages of Bosham and Fishbourne on the edge of glorious Chichester Harbour.

Looking north over the Arun Valley

walk 15

Start

Arundel Station. Approx. 1 hour and 30 minutes from London Victoria

Distance

4¼ miles (6.8km)

Height gain

180 feet (55m)

Approximate time

2 hours

Route terrain

Pavement and parkland, woodland and riverside paths

OS maps

Explorer 121 (Arundel & Pulborough)

GPS waypoints

 TQ 024 064
Ⓐ TQ 013 073
Ⓑ TQ 012 080
Ⓒ TQ 011 086
Ⓓ TQ 018 077

Arundel Park and the River Arun

After crossing the River Arun, an opening uphill stretch leads from the town centre into Arundel Park. There are superb views as you descend into a dry valley and this is followed by beautiful woodland walking beside Swanbourne Lake. On the final leg, you keep along an embankment which follows the River Arun around a long bend, with magnificent views of Arundel's skyline, dominated by the castle, church and Roman Catholic cathedral. Note that dogs are not allowed in Arundel Park.

 Leaving the station, walk down the approach road and onto the main road (pavement left) heading towards the castle. Cross the road before a large roundabout and keep ahead for ¼ mile along The Causeway and then Queen Street to reach the River Arun. Cross the bridge, keep ahead at the crossroads and start the climb up High Street passing the war memorial and curving left alongside the castle walls. Continue past St Nicholas' church on your right and the Roman Catholic cathedral on your left.

Just beyond St Philip's primary school (also on your left) turn right up an estate road into Arundel Park, marked by a public right of way signpost Ⓐ. Go through a kissing-gate at the park lodge and head gently uphill, keeping to the road and ignoring two left-hand forks.

Turn right at a waymark Ⓑ post in front of the 18th-century Hiorne Tower, and walk across the grass to a second waymark

Arundel Castle

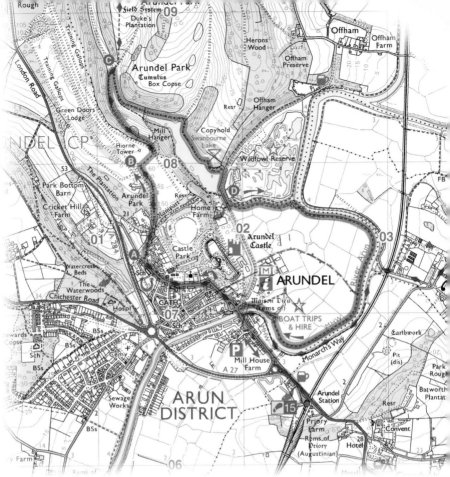

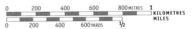

SCALE 1:25 000 or 2½ INCHES to 1 MILE 4CM to 1KM

post. Cross a gallop, continue briefly downhill with woodland on your right, then cross a stile and turn left onto a track. There are lovely views ahead as you descend through the trees to a crossways in the valley bottom.

Turn sharp right along the track **C** through the valley, continuing over a stile with glimpses of Swanbourne Lake through the trees on your right. Later you walk beside the lake to reach the café at Swanbourne Lodge; go through the gate here, and turn right onto Mill Road. Just before the bridge, bear left down a few steps at a public footpath sign. Continue beside the road bridge, climb a few more steps, and cross Swanbourne footbridge **D**.

Turn immediately left at a waymark post and follow a tree-lined path beside a stream to the River Arun. After climbing a stile, turn right onto the riverside embankment and follow the Arun around a sweeping right-hand bend. Three kissing-gates punctuate this section, and there are delightful views of Arundel castle, church and cathedral.

As you approach the town, bear right down the embankment and walk across Mill Road car park to reach Mill Road. Turn left past the remains of Blackfriars Dominican Friary; then, at the bridge, turn left into Queen Street and retrace your outward journey back to the start.

walk 16

Start

Fishbourne Station.
Approx. 1 hour 45
minutes from London
Victoria

Distance

5¼ miles (8.4km)

Height gain

Negligible

Approximate time

2½ hours

Route terrain

Flat tracks and field
paths

OS maps

Explorer 120
(Chichester)

GPS waypoints

SU 835 050
Ⓐ SU 829 047
Ⓑ SU 814 043
Ⓒ SU 809 039
Ⓓ SU 829 036
Ⓔ SU 838 045
Ⓕ SU 837 046

Fishbourne and Bosham

There is plenty of historic interest, as well as wide views and fresh breezes, on this flat walk across pasture and marshland fringing the creeks and inlets of Chichester Harbour. The walk starts and passes close to the remains of the Roman palace at Fishbourne, renowned for its outstanding mosaics and well worth a short detour; and visits the delightful village of Bosham, with its Saxon church and picturesque quayside.

Walk off the platform at Fishbourne Station to the level-crossing and turn right along Salthill Road following this to the T-junction with the main road (A259). On the way you will pass Roman Way (left) leading to the Roman Palace which deserves a visit at the end of the walk.

Turn right along the main road with good pavements on both sides. Keep ahead for about 400 yds and, immediately past new housing, bear left into Old Park Lane, and continue until the lane bears left at a junction Ⓐ.

Keep ahead along a signposted farm track beside a line of trees. Pass a fingerpost and turning on the left, and follow the track as it bears right to a T-junction. Keep ahead along the sign-posted field-edge path beside a hedge on your right. Keep ahead past a signposted turning on your right, now with glimpses of large glasshouses through hedgerow trees on the right.

Beyond the trees the path continues ahead, now following a ditch and hedge on your left-hand side. Finally, the path meets Walton Lane at a bend in the road, beside the entrance to Rectory Farm Ⓑ.

Keep ahead onto the road, ignoring all turnings, until you reach the Berkeley Arms. Opposite the pub, turn left down an enclosed tarmac footpath; cross a residential road and keep ahead as the path joins another residential road at a bend. After 100 yds turn right, and walk down Harbour Road to the end.

Turn right Ⓒ and either follow Shore Road (flooded at

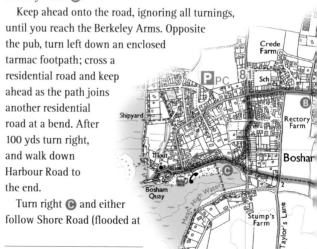

each high tide) or the higher sea wall path to Bosham Lane. Take your time to explore the narrow lanes of the village; *if Shore Road is covered by the tide pass along the lane in front of the café to the church*, but if the tide permits it is possible to follow the Shore Road around to Bosham Quay and enjoy the absolute picture that the harbour, the green and the church presents. When you've completed your stroll around Bosham retrace your steps to **C**. Bear right along the edge of the green for 100 yds to a second bench seat, and turn immediately left across the grass to a lane. Cross over, and keep ahead along the narrow, signposted footpath to cross Taylor's Lane.

Climb a few steps and continue across a field. Cross a drainage channel on the far side and turn right over a ditch; then, at a public footpath sign, turn left along a track. Later the path bears right, loops around a cottage, and continues along the left-hand side of a field.

After going through a hedge gap, keep ahead along an enclosed path and pass beside a barrier onto Park Lane.

Cross over and continue across the fields until the path becomes enclosed and reaches a T-junction and fingerpost **D**.

Turn right along the grassy track for 300 yds as far as the next fingerpost; then, turn left to follow a broad grassy track along the right-hand edge of a field. Keep ahead through an area of scrub, and continue across the marsh. Now the path bears left and runs beside Fishbourne Channel before diving left through a hedge gap and up onto the sea wall. From here there are good views of Chichester cathedral, across the water on your right.

At length the sea wall bears left, and runs between reedbeds. Next, turn right down a few steps, marked by a fingerpost, cross the reedbeds and several footbridges before skirting a millpond and emerging onto Mill Lane **E**.

Turn left up the lane to the Bull's Head **F**, then left again along the A259 and follow signs back to the station or detour to visit the Roman Palace.

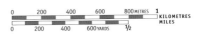

SCALE 1:25000 or 2½ INCHES to 1 MILE 4CM to 1KM

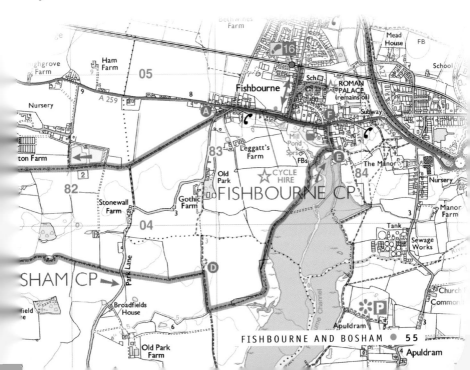

Start

Billingshurst Station. Approx. 1 hour 15 minutes from London Victoria

Distance

6¾ miles (10.8km)

Height gain

195 feet (60m)

Approximate time

3 hours

Route terrain

Field and canal side paths

OS maps

Explorer 134 (Crawley & Horsham)

GPS waypoints

TQ 087 251
Ⓐ TQ 072 254
Ⓑ TQ 062 244
Ⓒ TQ 058 243
Ⓓ TQ 058 245
Ⓔ TQ 066 255
Ⓕ TQ 069 271
Ⓖ TQ 076 268
Ⓗ TQ 080 262

The Wey and Arun Canal from Billingshurst

There is hardly anything in the way of a gradient in this interesting walk by the upper reaches of the River Arun. The path runs between the river and the towpath of the old Wey and Arun Canal.

Before the coming of the railway, Billingshurst was a busy staging-post on the road between Bognor and London, and several large inns lined the main street. While the railway dealt an initial blow to the fortune of Billingshurst, it later restored its prosperity when commuters began to settle in and around the village. This development has accelerated in recent years, and the walk sets off through the pleasant modern housing that now reaches out to the A29 bypass.

From the entrance to the station turn right into Station Road, just up from the level-crossing and keep with it all the way to the T-junction with Alicks Road. Turn right in the Haywards Heath direction and take the next left, the A272, West Street; then left at the roundabout into Newbridge Road East, and go across the footbridge over the bypass. Continue along the redundant highway past Bridgewaters Farm and bear left to join the footpath by the side of the A272. At Lordings Road (B2133) turn left to pass the Victorian postbox and the pantiled Limeburners Inn. About 50 yds after the pub, turn right Ⓐ on to the drive to Guildenhurst Manor.

After 100 yds leave the drive to the left through a kissing-gate. A wooden wicket gate now leads you diagonally across a paddock to a gate near its right-hand corner. The enclosed footpath now bears right through a second gate to skirt paddocks and crosses a footbridge at the corner. From here, follow the signposted zigzag left, then right, and continue down the signposted path between hedging and fencing to reach a large pond. Turn right, and follow the water's edge around to the left until you cross the concrete bridge over the outlet stream. Bear right after this to follow the new-born River Arun on a delightful path that gives a distant view of the church at Wisborough Green. Go through a damp meadow full of buttercups to come to a stile just before electricity lines. Keep ahead for 50 yds after this, before bearing left **B** to climb with the cables overhead to the top of the wood.

Turn right on to a grassy path that follows the edge of the wood westwards, enjoying the wide view of richly wooded hills with no habitation in sight until Frithwood Farm appears on the left. Continue to skirt the wood as the path drops to a gateway, beyond which the footpath divides **C**. Keep right to follow the path that curves right to reach the footbridge and kissing-gate at Lording's Lock. This lock (also known as Orfold Lock) is the top lock of six and from here the barges had to travel another 67 miles to reach London Bridge. The canal crosses the river on an aqueduct just

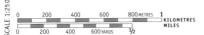

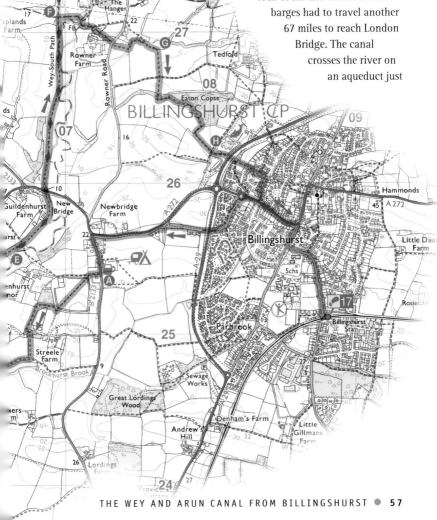

Wey and Arun Canal

gates have been restored. Cross the River Arun at a sluice and climb the path to the top, bearing left through a farmyard to reach Rowner Road. Cross it to a stile. Cross a field to a footbridge in the left-hand corner. Turn left and walk along the edge of a field to reach a signpost at a junction by three metal gates. Do not go through the gates but keep the wire fence to the left for 100 yds to a signpost **G**.

Turn right across the field to the signpost and stile opposite. Cross a lane and then a meadow; go through a belt of trees and then, before the second gate, turn left at the signpost onto an enclosed footpath by the side of Eaton Copse. Turn right at the footpath sign by the end of the copse and continue through a wooded tunnel for 100 yds. Now turn left over a stile and follow the left-hand hedge down the side of an open field towards new housing.

At a crossways by trees **H**, take the right-hand stile and, keep ahead through woodland to reach the bypass.

Cross the road to the footpath opposite, and after a few paces join another path. Keep left and shortly, as the path bends left, go straight on through woodland to pass a children's play area. Bear left to join Arun Road and follow this as it bends right, and then turn left to an 'Arun Road Garages' sign, then right beside the first garage on the right to follow a tarmac path through to the main road. On reaching this, turn left to retrace your outward route back to the Station.

north of the lock, where an information board explains the details and continuing restoration.

Go over the stile after the lock **D** and keep ahead along the left bank of the old canal (if you prefer you can follow a meandering riverside path). Parts of the canal are infilled as the right of way cuts across a wide loop of the river. The path continues over a stile and turns left as it runs between canal and river. After a wooden footbridge, keep ahead **E** – do not cross Guildenhurst Bridge to the right over the Arun – and follow the canal to Newbridge.

Cross the road and continue by the canal – even if you fail to spot a kingfisher, dragonflies and herons should be seen somewhere along this section. The lift bridge at Northlands Farm does not look as though it is operated often, but the memorial stone close by is poignant – 'a place for kingfishers to rest'.

Turn right **F** at a canal bridge by Rowner Lock, just before the electricity pylon spanning the canal. Here lock

Limpsfield

An attractive route following part of the Greensand Way to the Kent border and later joining a section of the Vanguard Way. The directions must be followed closely between Ⓔ and Ⓕ. There are a few descents and a couple of steep climbs through areas of woodland.

Start	Hurst Green Station. Approx. 30 minutes from London Bridge and 40 minutes from London Victoria
Distance	8½ miles (13.6km)
Height gain	655 feet (200m)
Approximate time	4 hours
Route terrain	Pavement and undulating woodland paths
OS maps	Explorer 147 (Sevenoaks & Tonbridge)

GPS waypoints

- TQ 399 513
- Ⓐ TQ 406 518
- Ⓑ TQ 416 521
- Ⓒ TQ 420 521
- Ⓓ TQ 436 522
- Ⓔ TQ 435 513
- Ⓕ TQ 429 513
- Ⓖ TQ 429 508
- Ⓗ TQ 422 507
- Ⓙ TQ 416 516

Stride away from the front of the station to reach Greenhurst Lane; turn left and over the railway keep ahead along Hurstlands, following the road as it curves left through housing. Shortly after the turning for Home Park where the pavement on the right-hand side of the road ends, turn right on a tarmac path between houses. After crossing a residential road and passing through another section of housing the path emerges onto a playing field. Follow the right edge of the field and where there is a gap in the line of trees pass through to pick up a tree-lined path between playing fields. This leads to Pollards Wood Road Ⓐ; go left. Just before the road curves right, turn left at a public footpath sign into woodland, along a steep, uphill path. At the driveway to a school turn right and then right again at the main road. At the T-junction turn left and then right into New Road and after a few paces join a path that veers right to cross Limpsfield Common.

The common lies on the Kent border on the Greensand Ridge and is dominated by woodland that is carpeted with bluebells in springtime. In the past few centuries grazing helped to keep the common as open heathland but a decline in this has encouraged scrub to appear and just a few patches of heath remain. The National Trust is now working to preserve these open areas and encourage wildlife to thrive here.

Keep ahead as the Greensand Way joins your path from the left and follow it uphill. At a tarmac track bear left to cross a road and continue along the path at a bridleway sign to pass the edge of a golf course and come out at Chapel Road Ⓑ. Turn left, cross the main road (the B269) and turn left into Ridlands Lane. Continue down the lane and turn right at a public bridleway sign Ⓒ. Go through a gap in the trees on the right to pass in front of a barn and join a driveway. At the road turn left

and keep ahead as the footpath becomes enclosed and veer away from the road. You are now on the Greensand Way. Cross a lane, turn left at the Carpenters Arms pub and cross another lane, all the while following Greensand Way waymarkers, bearing left at a waymarked post. Soon you will enter Titsey Foundation woodland where there is a good mix of silver birch and pine. Keep ahead until you reach a five-way path junction – just ahead, a few paces farther, is a stone marking the spot where the Greensand Way is equidistant between Hamstreet in Kent and Haslemere in Surrey – turn sharp right at the junction **D** and keep along the straight, woodland path, passing beside a gate to a road. Cross the road and continue along the public footpath opposite, which initially runs beside a metal fence, and then descends through the trees.

Keep ahead downhill as the path narrows to arrive at a tarmac driveway. Turn right along this **E** and at a fork bear left along the waymarked Tandridge Border Path, bearing left

again at the next fork to continue downhill.

Near here is a woodland house called The Cearne where D.H. Lawrence would visit when he was in the area. The house became a meeting place for writers and artists as well as Russian refugees.

At a track bear right past another waymarked post and Scearn Bank Farm, and where the road ascends through trees bear left along a narrow path, which shortly descends to a lane on the edge of Scearn Bank woodland **F**.

Woodland near Scearn Bank

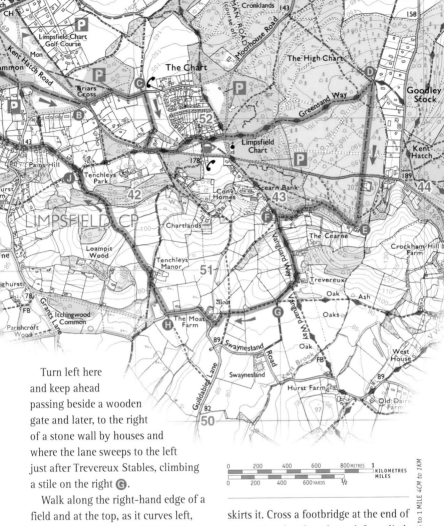

Turn left here and keep ahead passing beside a wooden gate and later, to the right of a stone wall by houses and where the lane sweeps to the left just after Trevereux Stables, climbing a stile on the right G.

Walk along the right-hand edge of a field and at the top, as it curves left, look out for where you climb a stile on the right. Continue along the left edge of the field and in the corner hop over another stile and immediately turn right along the enclosed path. Climb another stile on to a lane, opposite which is a pond. Turn right, past Moat Farm and its nearby cottages, and just before Chartlands climb a stile on the right H and walk along the left edge of a field. Climb a stile in the corner and go over a plank footbridge then bear right across grass to join a gravel track to the left of a house.

Keep ahead, and although the footpath passes through a garden there is an alternative path to the left that skirts it. Cross a footbridge at the end of this enclosed path and turn left to climb over a stile. Keep along the left-hand edge of the field, hop over a stile in the top left corner to enter woodland and follow the path, past the backs of houses, to a gravel track.

Turn left J, and rejoin the Greensand Way and a few paces farther, at a path junction, turn right along the tarmac road opposite Arden Lodge and continue all the way to a road.

Cross the road and join the footpath opposite, which passes a house and descends along the edge of woodland, and climb a stile on to a road A. From here, reverse your outward route to return to Hurst Green Station. ●

Witley to Haslemere via Chiddingfold

Start

Witley Station.
Approx. 1 hour from
London Waterloo

Distance

7¼ miles (11.6km)

Height gain

490 feet (150m)

Approximate time

3½ hours

Route terrain

Lanes, woodland and
grassy paths

OS maps

Explorer 133
(Haslemere &
Petersfield)

GPS waypoints

- SU 948 379
- Ⓐ SU 950 373
- Ⓑ SU 954 369
- Ⓒ SU 958 358
- Ⓓ SU 942 344
- Ⓔ SU 936 344
- Ⓕ SU 926 336
- Ⓖ SU 906 326

A linear route following a beautiful valley of rolling hills and streams, passing the pretty village of Chiddingfold and belts of woodland before joining the Serpent Trail in Haslemere. Haslemere Station is the first stop south of Witley.

From Witley Station car park walk down Station Approach and at the crossroads turn right. After 600 yds turn left at a public footpath sign Ⓐ and climb a stile, then cross a paddock to climb another one. Keep ahead through a belt of trees to climb a stile and head half left, across a field, to a stile by a hedge gap. Hop over the stile and go across the plank footbridge into the next field, heading for the left of farm buildings opposite, and climb another stile.

Bear left past Noddings Farm and at the public footpath signpost turn right to climb a stile Ⓑ. Keep initially along the right-hand edge of the field, and then head downhill towards a metal gate. This is a beautiful stretch of the walk with rolling hills and green pastures.

Go through the gate, cross a narrow field and hop over the stile and cross an earth bridge to enter woodland of Hartsgrove Hanger. Cross another earth bridge and head gently uphill, go through a kissing-gate, then stay along the right-hand edge of a field towards the backs of houses. In the field corner go through a kissing-gate and then along an enclosed path to a road. Turn left and follow the road as it curves right and keep ahead at a junction. Turn right into Coxcombe Lane Ⓒ and at the end is Chiddingfold's pretty village green with its pond, church and The Crown pub. For 300 years the village was famed for its glassmaking and most of the properties around its green date from the 14th to 16th centuries. Turn right passing to the left of St Mary's Church, and then turn right along Mill Lane.

Ignore the public footpath signs to the right and keep ahead past Upper Sydenhurst along the tarmac bridleway, which skirts the edge of woodland. The path bears left in front of a gate to

Village pond, Chiddingfold

Hollyhurst and runs beside a wire fence. Keep ahead all the way to a lane and turn left ⓓ.

Just before the road curves left over a bridge, keep ahead at a bridleway sign and after passing farm buildings turn left over a stile ⓔ.

Bear half-right across the field, hop over a stile along the wooden fence, and cross the next field, then keep along the left-hand edge. Ignore the stile on the left and climb the stile in the field corner beside a yellow waymarked post.

A few paces farther, keep ahead at another yellow waymarker and continue along the edge of Frillinghurst Wood. Cross a wooden footbridge and head uphill and at a fork by a public footpath sign bear left through a copse, following the yellow waymarked posts, to continue along the left edge of a field. At the path junction, go through a

hedge gap on the left and bear right to another set of signposts in front of a fishing lake ⓕ.

Turn left and follow the path as it curves right to skirt the edge of the lake and passes to the right of farm buildings. Cross a lane and go through the kissing-gate opposite beside Holdfast Cottage. Keep along the right edge of a field, go through a kissing-gate and turn right past houses, along an enclosed path. Go through another kissing-gate into Swan Barn Farm, an area rich in wild flowers and managed by the National Trust. The path then follows the right-hand edge of a series of fields linked by kissing-gates, plank footbridges and steps, to enter Witley Copse and Mariners Rewe at a National Trust sign. The path continues to the right of a wire fence and bears left at a fork to reach a three-way footpath sign next to a National

Wooded valley near Hartsgrove Hanger

accessible after the London to Portsmouth railway opened in 1859. Many well-known artists and writers liked to visit including George Eliot, Alfred Lord Tennyson, Conan Doyle and George Bernard Shaw.

Look out for a plaque on the town hall dedicated to General James Oglethorpe, a local MP from 1722 to 1754, who founded the colony of Georgia in the United States of America.

Trust one on the edge of the copse. Keep ahead joining the Serpent Trail, which was opened in 2005. Cross a wooden footbridge, go through the gate and head straight across a field. Go through a hedge gap and keep ahead through a gate. Bear right to join a gravel track and follow this all the way to Haslemere's main road **G**.

The town grew when it became more

Turn right here and keep ahead, following signs to the station in Haslemere where you should catch the train one stop back to Witley or on to Waterloo.

SCALE 1:27777 or 2¼ INCHES to 1 MILE 3.6CM to 1KM

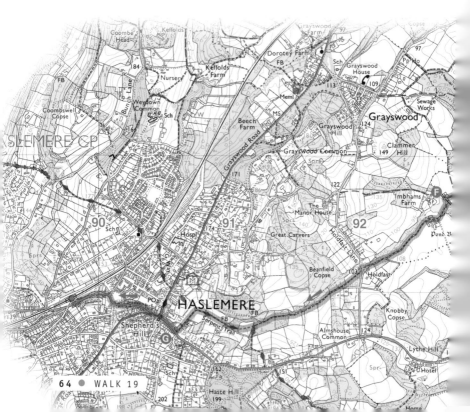

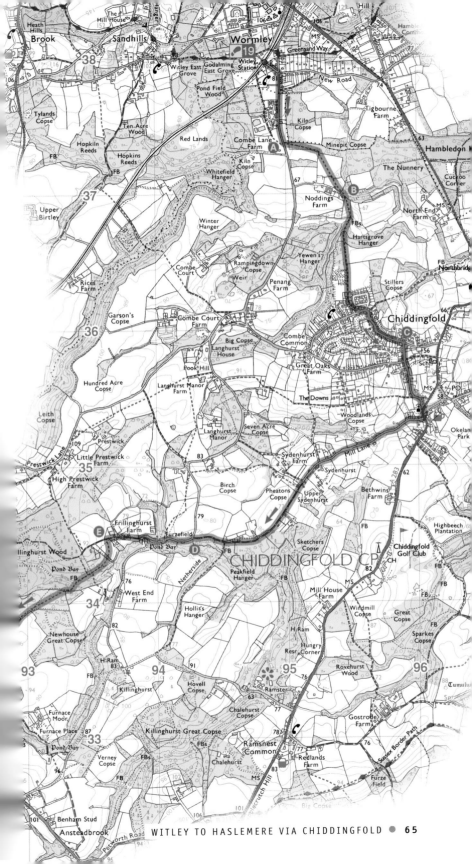

walk 20

Gomshall to the Abingers

Start

Gomshall Station. Approx. 1 hour 5 minutes from London Waterloo and 1 hour 10 minutes from London Bridge

Distance

8 miles (13km)

Height gain

755 feet (230m)

Approximate time

4 hours

Route terrain

Woodland paths and enclosed tracks, some quiet country lanes

OS maps

Explorers 145 (Guildford & Farnham) and 146 (Dorking, Boxhill & Reigate)

GPS waypoints

- TQ 088 478
- Ⓐ TQ 092 476
- Ⓑ TQ 112 482
- Ⓒ TQ 121 483
- Ⓓ TQ 126 461
- Ⓔ TQ 105 460
- Ⓕ TQ 091 470

There are some excellent views – and plenty of stiles – along this walk which covers a mix of farms, woodland and heath beneath the North Downs escarpment. After a gradual ascent to Abinger Roughs the route crosses the Tilling Bourne and then climbs once more. There are some splendid views across the valley and a couple of great pubs in equally scenic settings.

Turn left out of the station and walk through the car park into Station Road and pass under the railway bridge and after 500 yds turn left along an enclosed track (Beggars Lane) at a public byway signpost Ⓐ.

After 200 yds look out for a narrow, uphill path through trees on the right and follow this, through a gate and along an enclosed path with some good views on the left over the valley towards Netley Heath. Cross a lane and pick up the path opposite to go through a gate and then keep ahead on a gradual ascent, following blue waymarkers to enter the woodland of Broomy Downs.

At a junction of paths keep ahead along the main bridleway, through an area called Abinger Roughs, following an undulating route through the trees to pass a memorial to Samuel Wilberforce. This marks the spot where the son of the abolitionist was killed after falling from his horse in 1873. At a road cross over and follow the bridleway (not the footpath to the right of it), Ⓑ along an enclosed path with fields to the left.

At the junction of paths just past Park Farm bear right uphill along a footpath that goes across grass towards woodland Ⓒ. Go through a kissing-gate into Deerleap Wood and follow the enclosed path past a church, all the way to the A25 at Wotton. The Saxon church stands alone overlooking the North Downs and has some unusual carved heads around the porch door including those of King John and Archbishop Stephan Langton. Inside is the tomb of John Evelyn, the diarist.

Cross the road and head through the car park beside The Wotton Hatch pub then climb a stile and make for the top right corner of the field to climb another stile. Follow the sunken path downhill to cross the Tilling Bourne stream and ascend the other side. Go over another stile and follow the path as it heads uphill through Damphurst Wood, ignoring side paths. At a T-junction before a series of weirs, turn left and continue along a wide path and hop over a stile to reach a path crossing .

Turn right and cross an old stone bridge over the Tilling Bourne and bear left along an uphill track, to a road. Turn right along the road and look out for where you join a path on the right, beside a sunken bridleway. At a road turn right, and then first left along a tarmac lane. At the T-junction turn right to pass The Abinger Hatch pub, which is in a peaceful spot, opposite the church and the tiny village green. Turn left by a public footpath sign in front of the church, go through the lychgate and pass to the left of the church to go through a gate and along an enclosed path that skirts Abinger Manor and its motte. Go through a kissing-gate and keep ahead, initially along the left edge of a field, after which the path becomes a track and curves left before Raikes Farm. At a fork bear left and continue beside a wire fence along a narrow path. Go down steps and at a lane, turn left.

At the end of this lane is The Volunteer, another charming pub with an attractive garden, but to continue

Woodland at Gomshall

the walk, turn right at a bridleway sign **E** before reaching the pub. Follow this as it swings right at a set of iron gates, and continues along the right-hand edge of a field. Cross a track and bear left along the bridleway and at the next three-way signpost, turn left to join a public footpath. Keep beside the wire fence on the left, climb a stile and maintain direction as the path descends across farmland. Climb another stile and continue along a narrow enclosed path to hop over a stile to a road.

Cross the road and go over the stile ahead then keep ahead across a field, passing to the left of two large oak trees and, at the field edge, by a public footpath signpost, turn right, **F**.

The path curves left and passes a stile to reach a bridleway where you turn left, through a hedge gap and head diagonally right to the corner of the field. Bear left along a track and at the T-junction by Southbrook Farmhouse, turn right along a gravel bridleway and follow this as it veers to the right and crosses a stream before reaching the A25.

Turn left to go under the railway bridge and return to where the walk began.

SCALE 1:25 000 or 2½ INCHES to 1 MILE 4CM to 1KM

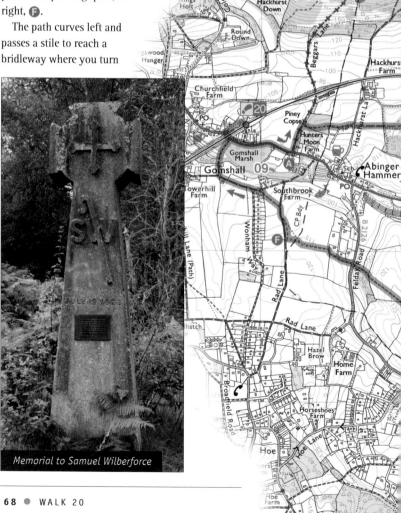

Memorial to Samuel Wilberforce

The Abinger Hatch pub

walk 21

Box Hill

Start

Boxhill and
Westhumble Station.
Approx. 50 minutes
from London Victoria
and London Waterloo

Distance

11¾ miles (18.8km)

Height gain

1,790 feet (545m)

Approximate time

6 hours

Route terrain

Lanes, tracks and
woodland paths with
some steep climbs and
descents

OS maps

Explorer 146 (Dorking,
Box Hill & Reigate)

GPS waypoints

  TQ 167 518
Ⓐ TQ 163 514
Ⓑ TQ 158 512
Ⓒ TQ 139 504
Ⓓ TQ 140 515
Ⓔ TQ 147 542
Ⓕ TQ 161 538
Ⓖ TQ 170 533
Ⓗ TQ 178 532
Ⓙ TQ 184 516
Ⓚ TQ 179 511

The greater part of this route is through woodland that is recovering well from the hurricane of 1987. It is advisable to pack a picnic and to take mud-proof footwear, unless the weather has been unusually dry. In the final section of the walk, after Mickleham, there are some quite demanding climbs.

Walk away from the station and bear left along Westhumble Street to cross over the railway. Curve left on Chapel Lane to pass an impressive arch (right) and look for a hidden enclosed path off left after passing the entrance to Pilgrim Way. Keep with the fence and tall hedge-lined path, cross a lane to continue on the enclosed path opposite, eventually opening into a narrow pasture. Follow the obvious grassy path straight ahead to a belt of trees concealing a path junction with the North Downs Way Ⓐ; turn right.

Several footpaths cross the track, but keep on the North Downs Way after it curves south for about 200 yds, then at a signposted crossing of tracks Ⓑ turn right along a bridleway off the North Downs Way into Ashcombe Wood. After another 200 yds uphill, a footpath sign directs you to the left and further uphill.

The path continues steadily uphill through woods, latter flattens out and becomes a metalled, then concrete road passing Denbies Farm. There may be deer in enclosures on your left. Pass straight on through a gateway to the public highway.

Carry straight on along the quiet lane to reach Ranmore. A bridleway runs along the wide verge, where walking is easier than on tarmac. Pass the Victorian flint church at Ranmore, bear right at the main road – the bridleway is now on the right – and pass the National Trust car park on the left. Immediately after the three houses on the right (the third, called Fox Cottages, has pantiles and tall chimneys) there is a track with a sign to the youth hostel Ⓒ.

A few paces farther, bear left at a fork. This is a lovely stretch of a mile or so of woodland walking and then the roof and chimneys of Polesden Lacey can be seen over a clearing to the left. The house becomes hidden as the track drops down to the picturesque youth hostel, Tanner's Hatch Ⓓ, where a bridleway joins from the left.

Pass the hostel and continue downhill along a delightful track which reaches the bottom of an open valley, and keep ahead at a fork by a blue waymarked post in the Connicut Lane direction.

View from Box Hill

Walk along the track to pass beneath a balustraded bridge carrying an estate road over the track. The climb is steep for a while through Freehold Wood.

Turn right onto Polesden Road, where there is a parallel bridleway on the left. Where Polesden Road meets another road, cross straight over to walk up a track with paddocks to the left. This track, known as Admiral's Road, skirts Great Bookham and once it has crossed another bridleway it becomes a field edge path, narrow and enclosed for a short distance before meeting a track into Norbury Park.

Turn right onto this track ⓔ and go down the hill to pass Roaringhouse Farm. Keep straight on after the red brick farmhouse up a bridleway which climbs steeply to start with and then descends abruptly. Keep straight ahead when a track crosses the bridleway and continue up through a group of yew trees. The bridleway meets another track at a blue waymarker. Bear left and walk along the track a short way to another junction with a picnic site, an information board about Norbury Park and a signpost. Keep ahead with fencing to your right.

The bridleway passes the drive to Norbury Park house, the home of Dr Marie Stopes at the time of her death in 1957. The bridleway joins the drive from the house, before leaving it to the right. Pass another entrance to the house and bear right, keeping beside the fencing. The route follows the perimeter fence to a signpost on the right to a viewpoint ⓕ. It is worth the short detour to visit this spot where a seat has been placed so that the fine view southwards to Box Hill may be enjoyed in comfort. The viewpoint must be one of the few good things to have followed the 1987 hurricane, which opened up the vista.

Returning to the bridleway, this descends steeply to reach a surfaced track. Remain on the track until it swings sharply to the left. Keep straight on here on a narrow path. Turn right when the track meets a lane at the bottom, to cross a bridge over the River Mole to the main road. Take care when crossing this to the road opposite, which leads to Mickleham.

Turn left immediately past the church onto a driveway to Eastfield Cottage ⓖ. At a gate take the footpath over the stile to the right. This path through the woods soon begins to climb. Bear right at a fork and note the remains of a wall of dressed flint on the right. Go straight over Mickleham Downs Road. At the top of the following climb, the path swings to the right and begins to descend through a grove of yews. In the middle of these it swings right again **H** and then suddenly the view opens up ahead. There is a seat here. The path then begins a slippery descent to Juniper Bottom, or Happy Valley. Although steps have been cut for the latter part of the way, great care has to be taken initially, especially after wet weather. Cross the road at the bottom to enter Juniper Bottom.

The final part of the walk is through a valley flanked by rich woodland that gradually encroaches on the track as it climbs. Posts with numbers denote stages of a National Trust nature trail. Almost at the top of Juniper Bottom, at post 14 **J**, turn right to leave the bridleway. Level walking follows through the woods; you may see deer. At a clearing bear right to find the National Trust Box Hill car park. Walk with your back to the National Trust Information Centre at Fort Cottages, which take their name from a stronghold and ammunition store built here in the late 19th century, and turn right to the viewpoint and triangulation pillar **K**. The view southwards is spectacular, with the ground dropping away almost sheer to the River Mole some 400ft below. Descend to the right of the viewpoint and turn right onto the

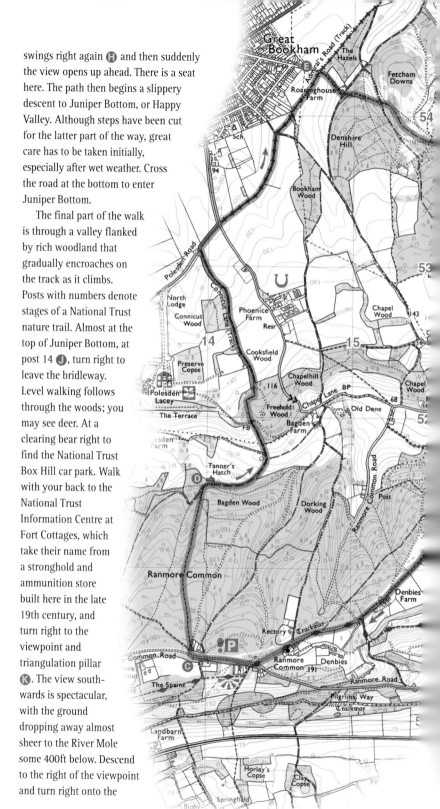

footpath and at a yellow North Downs Way waymarker turn left down steps.

At a waymarked post turn left to go steeply downhill through a group of yews. Steps have been cut into this path. Soon the River Mole can be glimpsed below, and you will see a signpost giving the choice of crossing the river either by stepping stones or a footbridge. The former method, bearing left, is more fun and offers the shorter route. Go up the track on the other side to the main road – the path from the footbridge rejoins here.

Take great care in crossing the dual carriageway. There is a track almost directly opposite which passes below the railway and then into the Denbies Wine estate. At the track crossways **A** turn right back to the station.

22 Great Kimble

Field paths and tracks; pedestrian crossing over railway

 2 miles (3.2km)

 1½ hours

23 Marlow & the Thames

Lanes, riverside and meadow paths

 3½ miles (5.6km)

 1½ hours

24 Goring

Undulating field and woodland paths

 5¼ miles (8.4km)

 2½ hours

25 Windsor & Eton

Riverside and meadow paths

 5½ miles (8.8km)

2½ hours

26 Chesham and Little Missenden

Undulating downland, woodland and field paths

9 miles (14.4km)

4½ hours

27 Lardon Chase, Moulsford and Streatley

Downland tracks and Thames path

 11½ miles (18.4km)

 5½ hours

Chalfont St Giles

Berkshire, Buckinghamshire & Oxfordshire

Only 30 miles or so to the west and north west of London lie the glorious beech-clad Chiltern Hills. Perfect for exploring on foot in any season – but particularly in the autumn when the leaves turn from dark green to deep brown to create a dazzling mosaic – this 308 square-mile designated Area of Outstanding Natural Beauty represents some of the best walking country in the south of England. With miles of peaceful beech woodland, rolling green hills and an assortment of picturesque villages, it's hard to believe you can be this close to the capital.

Located at the far end of the Metropolitan Line, the town of Chesham is a good starting point for exploring the meandering byways and bridleways of the region's delightfully leafy eastern corner. It comes as something of a surprise to find the familiar London Underground logo greeting you on the platform as you exit the station.

Running through the heart of the Chilterns, the 85-mile Ridgeway National Trail offers miles of superb scenery and spectacular views. North of Princes Risborough, near the village of Great Kimble, the trail passes through the grounds of Chequers, the Prime Minister's official country residence.

The Goring Gap – the point at which the Ridgeway crosses the Thames – is a well-known geological landmark and a popular haunt of walkers. From here, heading downstream, the stately river links a variety of delightful country walks as it cuts through the glorious countryside of Oxfordshire, Berkshire and Buckinghamshire. Beyond the charming town of Marlow, a perfect spot for an easy riverside stroll, the skyline is dominated by that most iconic of British landmarks – the Round Tower of Windsor Castle.

Downland near Streatley

Great Kimble

This short walk, based on the quiet village of Kimble and a short stretch of the Ridgeway National Trail, is a good introduction to the many beauties of the Chiltern Hills. Beautiful beech woodlands make their presence felt, but so too do the rolling farmlands of the area.

🐾 Leave the station and turn right, soon entering an enclosed path running alongside the railway line. At a stile, enter a field and follow the right-hand edge to another stile in the far corner (ignore an intermediate stile on the right).

Go forward along another enclosed path which leads up steps to a road. Turn right, crossing the railway bridge and immediately go left down steps so that you are parallel to the railway line once more.

Two more stiles lead across a small paddock into a large arable field. Keep to the left-hand field margin, as far as a metal kissing-gate on the left. Through this, cross the railway line with great care.

In the next field, bear right along a grassy path to a stile in the far corner and then go up the next field alongside a small, elongated pond on the left, to a corner.

Cross a stile Ⓐ and bear half-right, aiming for the right-hand edge of a red-brick house in the distance. Beside the house, a stile gives on to an access driveway leading out to the A4010.

Cross the road with care and go on to a broad track opposite, but immediately bear right, along a branching track into scrub.

Bridleway, Great Kimble

The track leads out to a road (Cadsdean Road). Turn left and follow the road for about ¼ mile), taking care against approaching traffic.

Continue to a path on the left, signposted for the Ridgeway 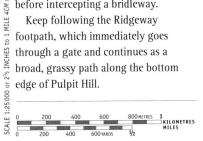B. Leave the road here, through a kissing-gate, and start up a long flight of steps, ending at another gate into a large field. Go forward across the field and, on the far side, enter a short stretch of scrub before intercepting a bridleway.

Keep following the Ridgeway footpath, which immediately goes through a gate and continues as a broad, grassy path along the bottom edge of Pulpit Hill.

After a short section of open pasture, the Ridgeway path climbs to another gate and rises a little farther to meet a sunken bridleway C. Turn left (signposted to Wolverton).

Go down the bridleway, which is flanked by beech, hawthorn, ivy, sycamore and field maple. The descending track becomes a surfaced lane, leading out to the A4010.

Turn right and cross the road with care, passing the Church of St Nicholas. After the church, at the Bernard Arms, turn left into Church Lane.

Immediately on reaching Great Kimble School, turn right along a signposted path leading across a narrow enclosure. In the next field, bear left and cross to the right-hand edge of the field.

Follow a waymarked route across small enclosures and pass a large fish-filled pond before crossing a stream. Go forward across the next field to a stile on the other side giving on to a railway crossing. Ignore this and turn right along the field boundary, retracing the outward route to Little Kimble Station.

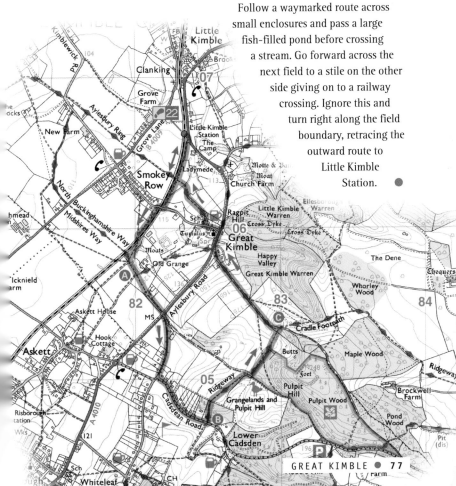

walk 23

Start

Marlow Station
Approx. 1 hour from
London Paddington

Distance

3½ miles (5.6km)

Height gain

Negligible

Approximate time

1½ hours

Route terrain

Lanes, riverside and
meadow paths

OS maps

Explorer 172 (Chiltern
Hills East)

GPS waypoints

- SU 855 865
- Ⓐ SU 850 863
- Ⓑ SU 838 844
- Ⓒ SU 836 848

Marlow and the Thames

Marlow is a hugely attractive town with its own rowing regatta and a history that goes back beyond the 'Domesday Book'; it is a lively, buzzing place and a perfect spot from which to begin an easy walk along the Thames Path.

Leave the station and walk to the entrance to Station Approach. Cross Lock Road, turn right and then left into Station Road to walk 400 yds to the junction with High Street Ⓐ. Cross carefully to the main entrance to Higginson Park opposite. Turn into the park and follow a diagonal path to reach the Thames. Turn right.

Eventually the surfaced Thames-side path breaks out into a large open meadow. Simply keep heading in the same direction, walking alongside the river.

Continue upriver passing modern housing built on Temple Mill Island – named after the Templars – and a short way on, as a weir is approached, leave the Thames Path by turning inland

The 12th-century church at Bisham

along a track **B** leading towards Low Grounds Farm.

At a double bend, leave the track by branching right on to a rough farm track heading back towards Marlow **C**.

Beyond a gate and stile, the track improves and soon becomes surfaced. Keep forward to a T-junction with Pound Lane, turn right and walk on to where it meets the High Street **A**. Retrace your outward route back to the railway station. ●

The Thames at Marlow

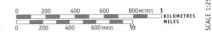

SCALE 1:25000 or 2½ INCHES to 1 MILE 4CM to 1KM

Goring

Start

Goring & Streatley Station. Approx. 50 minutes from London Paddington

Distance

5¼ miles (8.4km)

Height gain

625 feet (190m)

Approximate time

2½ hours

Route terrain

Undulating field and woodland paths

OS maps

Explorers 170 (Abingdon, Wantage & Vale of White Horse) and 171 (Chiltern Hills West)

GPS waypoints

SU 602 805
Ⓐ SU 602 808
Ⓑ SU 613 814
Ⓒ SU 625 818
Ⓓ SU 628 812
Ⓔ SU 633 807
Ⓕ SU 632 798
Ⓖ SU 605 806

Based in the south-western fringe of the Chilterns this walk follows an undulating route in an arc to the north, east and south of Goring, passing through a succession of attractive wooded areas. Near the end there are superb views looking across the Thames Valley to the Berkshire Downs.

Turn left out of the station and walk along Gatehampton Road, passing Reading Road (right), and opposite the High Street (left) turn right down a driveway, signposted Cleeve Ⓐ. Where the drive bends slightly right turn left along a fenced tarmac path to a road. Keep ahead through a modern housing area and where the road ends, continue along a tarmac path for a few paces, then turn right through a fence gap and cross a track.

Follow the waymarked path between fences to a stile, turn right and climb another one after a few paces (Chiltern Way). Follow the grassy path along the lower slopes of a field, with houses visible to the left, and make for another stile in the corner of the pasture. Avoid a stile on the left after a few steps and keep ahead alongside wooden panel fencing. Keep sloping woodland on the right, to emerge on to a lane Ⓑ. Turn right and almost immediately turn left, at a public footpath sign to Beech Lane and Woodcote, along a narrow, enclosed path, later keeping along the left edge of woodland. The path bears right to continue uphill through Wroxhills Wood to a crossroads of paths.

Keep ahead, following the obvious path through the trees. Keep in a fairly straight line, to emerge on to a track in the far corner of the wood. Turn right along this hedge- and tree-lined track and at the point where it becomes a tarmac drive, turn right Ⓒ, at a public footpath sign, along the track which heads straight across fields and descends to a waymarked stile. Do not climb the stile but turn left and continue gently downhill along a track to go through a metal gate on to a road. Turn left and after about 100 yds bear right Ⓓ along a track through Old Elvendon Wood. Head uphill to emerge from the trees, continue along a track to a road Ⓔ, cross the road and climb a stile opposite, at a public footpath sign. Bear slightly left and follow an obvious path across the field. On the far side pass through a hedge gap to continue between hedgerows. The path curves right and left, following the contours of the field on the right. Soon you re-enter woodland and descend to a track in the valley bottom. Cross this track, take the uphill path ahead to a house, then turn left along another track in front of the house and follow it as it curves right and continues to a lane **F**.

Turn right along the narrow lane, passing to the left of Coldharbour Farm and follow the lane towards Stapnall's Farm. When you see a sign for Chalkwood House on a tree, bear left to follow the bridleway to a wooden gate into woodland. Pass the remains of another bridlegate and then turn right down a wide path that falls gently through the mainly coniferous Great Chalk Wood. On reaching the waymarked gateway within these woods turn left (do not go through the gateway) and then keep right at the fork. Go straight over the wide crossing trackway and keep left at the nearby fork. At a grassy fork bear right, gradually descending to a waymarked kissing-gate. Go through the gate and continue ahead to the next kissing-gate leading out to an immense field.

Turn right up the field edge, remaining with this round the top corner and ignoring a kissing-gate. There are impressive views from this section.

Pass through the gap at the top of the hedgerow and continue along the head of the next field. At the corner of the pasture turn right and head diagonally across the playing fields to the wooden railing at the end of the line of cupressus **G**. Pass through this into an estate road. Go ahead, turn left, then right at a T-junction to a lane. Turn left to another junction beside The Queen's Arms and go left to return to the station. ●

SCALE 1:27777 or 2¼ INCHES to 1 MILE 3.6CM to 1KM

walk 25

Windsor and Eton

Start

Windsor & Eton Central or Riverside Stations. Approx. 40 minutes from London Paddington to Windsor & Eton Central and 1 hour from London Waterloo to Windsor and Eton Riverside

Distance

5½ miles (8.8km)

Height gain

Negligible

Approximate time

2½ hours

Route terrain

Riverside and meadow paths

OS maps

Explorer 160 (Windsor, Weybridge & Bracknell)

GPS waypoints

SU 967 769 (Central Station)
SU 968 772 (Riverside Station)
Ⓐ SU 980 774
Ⓑ SU 973 781
Ⓒ SU 968 782
Ⓓ SU 950 783
Ⓔ SU 949 779

Riverside meadows, the playing fields of Eton and views of Windsor Castle and Eton College are the main ingredients of this flat and easy walk. Towards the end there is a particularly memorable view of Windsor Castle rising majestically above the opposite bank of the Thames. Leave plenty of time to explore the many historic attractions of Windsor.

From the banks of the Thames, Castle Hill winds up to Windsor Castle, the largest castle in Britain and a royal residence for over 900 years. It was begun by William the Conqueror in the late 11th century as one of a chain of castles defending the approaches to London, but over the centuries successive monarchs have remodelled and added to it – notably Henry II (who rebuilt the original circular keep), Henry III, Henry VIII, Charles II and George IV. Much of its present appearance dates from a particularly extensive programme of restoration and rebuilding carried out by George IV in the early 19th century. St George's Chapel, begun by Edward IV in 1478, is a masterpiece of Perpendicular Gothic architecture and contains many royal tombs. Despite all the additions and modernisation, Windsor still retains the basic plan of a Norman castle, with its varied buildings grouped around the massive 12th-century (though much restored) shell keep that dominates all the views of the fortress.

Although the castle is inevitably the major draw, Windsor has other attractions, including an elegant 17th-century guildhall.

Across the river is Eton, whose attractive High Street leads to the red brick buildings of Eton College, founded by Henry VI in 1440 but, like Windsor Castle, added to over the centuries. Many Prime Ministers, from the Elder Pitt to David Cameron, have been educated there.

 Emerge from Central Station and walk along the approach to face the castle, then turn left to wind your way all the way down Thames Street to the pedestrianised bridge. From Riverside Station, turn right along Dachet Road and then second right into Thames Street to reach the pedestrianised bridge over the Thames that links Windsor and Eton, and with your back to the river and facing Windsor Castle, turn left down steps on to Thames Side to walk alongside the river. After passing the River House pub continue along a tarmac path between railings – Romney Walk – passing to the left of the station, and on meeting a tarmac track turn left along it to enter Crown Estate land. The track keeps alongside the railway line to reach a boatyard by Romney Lock.

Go through a kissing-gate and walk along the riverside path to follow the Thames around a right-hand bend, passing under a railway bridge and continuing towards a road bridge. To the right are fine views across Home Park to the castle. Just before the road bridge turn sharp right across the grass to reach the road at the end of white railings, turn sharp left to cross the bridge, continue along the road for about 100 yds and turn left Ⓐ down some steps onto a track. Turn left and follow it along the left edge of Datchet golf course, by trees and undergrowth bordering the river.

Windsor Castle on the Thames

across more playing fields to cross a wide flat bridge, then join a wide track along the left margin of the sports fields (ignore the footbridge) to reach two brick cottages. Bear left along the driveway to a T-junction, turn right and keep left along the fenced lane to pass beneath the railway. Immediately beyond, keep ahead along the narrow stony path. Dog-leg beneath the bypass bridge and then follow the rough lane away from the embankment on a low causeway across fields to reach a four-way, waymarked footpath junction.

In the far corner of the golf course, continue along a path to pass beneath a railway bridge. On the left is the Jubilee River, a flood channel completed in 2002. Go left over the next footbridge, just beyond the railway bridge, and through two galvanised kissing-gates. Pass to the left of a boathouse. Keep ahead along the tarmac track to a road, bear left along it and then continue along the path parallel to it. Opposite a public footpath sign turn left over a footbridge **B** to follow a clear, well-surfaced track across part of the playing fields of Eton College. Just in front of a brick bridge, turn sharp right to continue along the track which immediately curves to the left and passes through a kissing-gate by a lodge on to a road **C**.

For the shorter version of the walk, turn left along the road, passing Eton College and continue along Eton High Street to the pedestrianised bridge.

For the full walk, cross the road and go through a gate in the fence opposite, at a public footpath sign. Keep ahead

Turn left over a stile, cross a footbridge over Common Ditch and turn right across the meadow, keeping roughly parallel to the ditch on your right to reach a galvanised kissing-gate leading into a lane. Turn left and follow this around to The Greyhound pub about 200 yds away. Turn left and walk to the main road **D**. Turn right, cross the road and in a few paces take the signposted path on the left, the tarred route of National Cycle Route 4. Follow this straight across the lush meadows to reach the bank of the Thames **E**.

Turn left and follow the winding river for about 1 ¹/₂ miles back to the start, passing under both road and railway bridges again. The grand finale to the walk is the majestic view of Windsor Castle, its walls and towers rising above the opposite bank. On reaching the end of the meadows keep ahead, first along Brocas Street as far as the bottom end of Eton High Street. Turn right to cross the bridge back into Windsor. ●

Chesham and Little Missenden

From Chesham the route proceeds through a quiet, undulating and off-the-beaten-track landscape of rolling hills, dry valleys and woodland in the heart of the Chilterns. The halfway point is Little Missenden, a delightful village with an interesting church in the Misbourne valley. This is a long walk with some narrow and possibly overgrown paths between Little Missenden and Hyde Heath and plenty of ups and downs, but none of the uphill stretches are steep or lengthy.

Although much of the historic interest of Chesham, a traditional Chilterns furniture-making town, has disappeared through the process of modern redevelopment, there are still some handsome old buildings and attractive streets near the restored medieval church. The former town hall building was demolished in 1965 but part of it has recently been re-erected as a clock tower and makes a striking feature in the pedestrianised High Street.

 Exit the station and walk across the approach area, bearing left to walk down Station Road, passing East Street (left) to reach a T-junction with High Street. Turn right and walk to the war memorial in the centre of the town. Turn left to a roundabout and cross the road to enter a park. After a short distance turn left along a broad, straight, tarmac path above Scottowe's Pond on the left, towards the church. In front of the churchyard entrance turn right Ⓐ, at a public footpath sign, along a tarmac drive, later bearing slightly left off it to continue along a track into a field.

Keep along the left-hand edge of the field, beside trees on the left, and at the end of the field the path continues through trees to a stile. Climb it, keep ahead to climb over another stile – this part of the walk follows Chiltern Link waymarks – bear slightly left and head gently downhill across a field to go through a kissing-gate on to a lane. Cross this lane, climb the stile opposite and walk diagonally across a field to another stile. Climb over it and continue across the next field to climb a stile on to a lane. Turn right and, carefully following the Chiltern Link waymarks, ignore the first public bridleway sign to the left but at the second one, signposted to Herberts Hole and South Heath, turn left to climb over a stile on to a track Ⓑ.

Follow the track through the dry valley bottom of Herberts Hole, a section of the walk that has a decidedly remote feel.

Start
Chesham Station. Approx. 1 hour from Central London on the Metropolitan Line

Distance
9 miles (14.4km)

Height gain
575 feet (175m)

Approximate time
4½ hours

Route terrain
Undulating downland, woodland and field paths

OS maps
Explorer 181 (Chiltern Hills North)

GPS waypoints
- SP 960 016
- Ⓐ SP 957 015
- Ⓑ SP 944 020
- Ⓒ SP 924 024
- Ⓓ SP 923 020
- Ⓔ SP 914 017
- Ⓕ SU 920 989
- Ⓖ SU 929 990
- Ⓗ SP 931 002
- Ⓙ SP 946 011

At the point where the track ends, go through a metal gate, keep ahead to go through another gate and continue, by a hedge and wire fence on the right, to a third one. Go through the gate, continue along a track, between woodland on the left and a hedge on the right, and about 50 yds farther on, look out for a yellow waymark where you turn left into the woodland **C**. Follow an uphill path through the trees which bends to the right, then climb a stile on the edge of the wood on to a lane.

Turn left along the lane, ignore the first public footpath sign on the right to Redding's Farm, but at the second (half-hidden in a hedge and opposite a house), turn right **D** over a stile. Walk

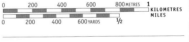

along the right-hand edge of fields, by a hedge and then a fence on the right, and where the fence ends keep ahead towards woodland. Go through a gap in the trees, but do not enter the next field. Instead bear slightly right on to a path that keeps along the left inside edge of some attractive woodland – several white arrows point the way – to a T-junction of paths. Turn left to continue along the right inside edge of the wood, go through a metal gate and, following the direction of a Circular Walk waymark, turn right along a tarmac drive between houses. At a yellow waymark turn left **E** along a hedge-lined path, passing to the right of a bungalow, climb a stile and continue along the left-hand edge of a field, by trees and a wire fence on the left. Climb another stile, keep along the right-hand edge of the next field, by a wire fence on the right, to climb a wooden fence in the field corner. Bear slightly left to cross the next field – there is no visible path – and climb a stile on to a road.

Turn left, and at public footpath and

Circular Walk signs turn right along a tarmac drive to The Hyde, passing to the left of a lodge. Where the drive turns right, bear slightly left to continue along a narrow path between trees and hedges to a stile. Climb it, continue along the right-hand edge of a field, by a fence on the right, climb another stile and keep in the same direction across the next field, heading down into a dip, then up again and bearing slightly right to climb a stile in the top right-hand corner. Cross a track and take the path ahead to enter woodland. The path – not very clearly defined – meanders along the left inside edge of the wood. Look out for where it turns left through a gap in a hedge into a field.

Turn right along the right-hand edge of the field and then, just before the field-edge bends right, turn half-left to follow a grassy path across the field. On the other side turn right to continue along the edge of Mantle's Wood on the

SCALE 1:25000 or 2½ INCHES to 1 MILE 4CM to 1KM

The church at Little Missenden

left, heading downhill. Ahead is a lovely view over a typical rolling Chilterns landscape. At the corner of the wood, follow the path to the left across the field to enter the wood and continue through it, heading uphill. Just before reaching the far edge, turn right at a crossroads of paths to head gently downhill; look out for a white arrow on a tree which points to the right. Cross a footbridge over a railway line, go down steps and walk along a path between trees and scrub, to emerge into a field. Keep ahead across the middle of the field, climb a stile, cross the busy A413 and climb a stile opposite to continue along the left-hand edge of a field, by trees on the left. Cross a footbridge over the River Misbourne and keep ahead to climb a stile in the field corner on to a road by Little Missenden church **F**.

The church is one of the oldest and most interesting in the Chilterns. It was founded in the late 10th century and there is Saxon, Norman and later work. The main features of interest are the murals, especially the 10ft-high one of St Christopher which was discovered in the 1930s. The village itself has a sleepy and secluded air, despite its proximity to the London–Aylesbury road, with a 17th-century manor house and some very distinguished Georgian houses. Turn left through the village, re-crossing the River Misbourne to rejoin the A413. Cross the road, take the

slip road opposite which bends right in front of a farm, and at a public footpath sign turn left over a stile **G**. On this next section the paths are narrow and likely to be overgrown in places. Climb another stile immediately ahead, continue along a path between wire fences, climb a stile and turn right. Turn left over a footbridge to re-cross the railway line and turn left again on the other side.

Do not turn right over the first stile but continue parallel to the railway and turn right over the next stile. Walk along a path between wire fences to another stile, climb it, continue ahead through the attractive Bray's Wood and climb a stile on to a road.

Turn right along the road through the modern residential area of Hyde Heath to a T-junction. Turn right, and at a public footpath and bridleway signs turn left **H** along a broad tarmac path across a common, continuing along a rough track past houses. Follow this track which bends to the right to keep along the right-hand edge of woodland, and just before reaching a metal gate, turn right along a hedge-lined path to enter White's Wood. Continue through the woodland, heading downhill, and on emerging from the trees keep along the right-hand edge of a field, by the edge of the wood on the right. In the field corner pass through a belt of trees and continue along a hedge-lined path to eventually reach a road to the right of a farm **J**.

Turn right along the road for one mile – there is a footpath – back to Chesham. On entering the town bear left along Church Street, cross the main road, keep ahead and turn left by the clock tower to walk along the pedestrianised High Street, finally turning right at Station Road to return to the station. ●

Lardon Chase, Moulsford and Streatley

walk 27

Start

Goring & Streatley Station. Approx. 50 minutes from London Paddington

Distance

11½ miles (18.4km)

Height gain

970 feet (295m)

Approximate time

5½ hours

Route terrain

Downland tracks and Thames Path

OS maps

Explorer 170 (Abingdon, Wantage & Vale of White Horse)

GPS waypoints

 SU 602 805
Ⓐ SU 594 807
Ⓑ SU 589 807
Ⓒ SU 581 814
Ⓓ SU 540 815
Ⓔ SU 544 826
Ⓕ SU 573 838
Ⓖ SU 576 836
Ⓗ SU 591 837
Ⓙ SU 593 836

After crossing the River Thames on the 19th century bridge the walk begins with a steep but short climb to the highest point above the Goring Gap where the Thames cuts through between the Chilterns and the Berkshire Downs to reveal magnificent views over the downs, Thames Valley and Chilterns. This is followed by a bracing walk across the sweeping, empty expanses of the Berkshire Downs and then a long descent down to the Thames, where the final stage is a delightful ramble along a lovely two-mile stretch of the river between Moulsford and Streatley. Although this is a long walk, much of it is across flat or gently undulating country and, except for the first one, all the climbs are gradual.

Turn left out of the station and walk along Gatehampton Road, passing Reading Road right, to reach the High Street. Here turn left and stroll easily down to the 19th century bridge linking Goring to Streatley on the west bank of the River Thames; a ferry was the only means of crossing before the bridge was built. Cross the bridge moving from Oxfordshire to Berkshire. Continue ahead to the turning for the lane to the church Ⓐ. Maintain direction along the High Street (B4009) where there are some particularly fine Georgian houses. Pass straight over at the crossroads in the Newbury direction and in just under 200 yds turn right Ⓑ past the Old School house along an uphill track. At a National Trust Lardon Chase sign, go through a gate and bear slightly left to follow a path steeply uphill across the open grassland to a gate at the top. From here there is a magnificent view over the Berkshire Downs, Thames Valley and Chilterns, with both Streatley and Goring churches below in the foreground and on either side of the Goring Gap. Do not go through the gate at the top but instead turn left in front of it, keep by the edge of trees on the right across the top of the chase and go through a gate to reach a car park. Walk through this towards the road, but before reaching it turn sharp right, at a public footpath sign, along an enclosed path which soon emerges on to the edge of a golf course. Cross the fairway and look for a track running between hedgerows. Continue down and across further fairways and near the bottom of the

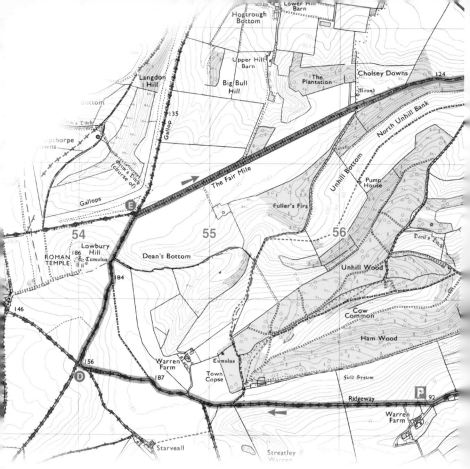

0	200	400	600	800 METRES	1
					KILOMETRES
					MILES
0	200	400	600 YARDS	½	

hillside look for a waymark. Bear slightly left to a footpath sign, cross a tarmac track and follow the path to the right of houses, to a lane **C**, here joining the Ridgeway.

Turn left along the lane, which is tree-lined for most of the way, through the bottom of the valley for one mile. At the entrance to Warren Farm, bear right at a Ridgeway sign to continue along a broad track for another 1¾ miles. The track ascends gently and is tree- and hedge-lined, then it emerges into open country, with grand views over the Berkshire Downs. Soon after it starts to descend you reach a junction with a byway. Continue on the Ridgeway,

keeping left at the immediate fork and, after 60 yds, at a crossroads and an 'Except for access' sign, turn right **D** to follow a waymarked byway.

After ¾ mile, at a junction of tracks, keep right **E** on a broad, grassy track and follow it for two miles across the downs. This is the 'Fair Mile', traditionally used by horseriders for gallops, from which there are some wonderful views, especially across the valley to the right to the wooded ridge of Unhill Wood. Eventually the two tracks converge and the route continues along a single hedge-lined track to a road **F**.

Turn right to head downhill – it is a busy road but there is a grass verge. Where the road curves slightly to the right, turn left **G**, at a public footpath

sign, on to a grassy track that heads gently uphill across a field. Keep immediately to the right of the narrow wooded embankment, passing beneath the line of pylons to the very end of the thicket. Here look right for a waymarked gap stile, go through this and in three paces go right along the narrow path between fence and trees. At the end of this turn right (do not enter the recreation ground) along a path between paddocks and housing to reach an estate road. Turn left along this, keep ahead at the junction and pick up the track beyond the wooden railings, walking ahead to a road in Moulsford **H**.

Turn right, take the first turn on the left, Ferry Lane, and follow it down between the buildings of the Beetle and Wedge Hotel to the riverbank **J**. Turn right to follow the riverside path for two miles to Streatley. This is a delightful stretch of the Thames, sometimes bordering woodland but mostly across open meadows, and passing Cleeve Lock; towards Streatley there is a particularly impressive view of the Goring Gap. Just after going through a gate into the final meadow, turn right to cross a footbridge on the edge of the meadow and continue along a shady tree-lined path which turns left and continues along a raised causeway into Streatley, passing to the left of the medieval church. Turn first right and then left by the church to reach a road . Turn left here, cross the bridge over the Thames once more and head back into Oxfordshire. Pass the Miller of Mansfield Hotel on the left and continue up the High Street to cross the railway bridge. Turn right at the T-junction and return to Goring and Streatley Station.

The River Thames at Streatley

Further Information

Walking Safety

Always take with you both warm and waterproof clothing and sufficient food and drink. Wear suitable footwear, such as strong walking boots or shoes that give a good grip over stony ground, on slippery slopes and in muddy conditions. Try to obtain a local weather forecast and bear it in mind before you start. Do not be afraid to abandon your proposed route and return to your starting point in the event of a sudden and unexpected deterioration in the weather.

All the walks described in this book will be safe to do, given due care and respect, even during the winter. Indeed, a crisp, fine winter day often provides perfect walking conditions, with firm ground underfoot and a clarity unique to this time of the year. The most difficult hazard likely to be encountered is mud, especially when walking along woodland and field paths, farm tracks and bridleways – the latter in particular can often get churned up by cyclists and horses. In summer, an additional difficulty may be narrow and overgrown paths, particularly along the edges of cultivated fields. Always ensure appropriate footwear is worn.

Walkers and the Law

The Countryside and Rights of Way Act (CRoW Act 2000) extends the rights of access previously enjoyed by walkers in England and Wales. Implementation of these rights began on 19 September 2004. The Act amends existing legislation and for the first time provides access on foot to certain types of land – defined as mountain, moor, heath, down and registered common land.

Where You Can Go
Rights of Way
Prior to the introduction of the CRoW Act, walkers could only legally access the countryside along public rights of way. These are either 'footpaths' (for walkers only) or 'bridleways' (for walkers, riders on horseback and pedal cyclists). A third category called 'Byways open to all traffic' (BOATs), is used by motorised vehicles as well as those using non-mechanised transport. Mainly they are green lanes, farm and estate roads, although occasionally they will be found crossing mountainous area.

Rights of way are marked on Ordnance Survey maps. Look for the green broken lines on the Explorer maps, or the red dashed lines on Landranger maps.

The term 'right of way' means exactly what it says. It gives a right of passage over what, for the most part, is private land. Under pre-CRoW legislation walkers were required to keep to the line of the right of way and not stray onto land on either side. If you did inadvertently wander off the right of way, either because of faulty map reading or because the route was not clearly indicated on the ground, you were technically trespassing.

Local authorities have a legal obligation to ensure that rights of way are kept clear and free of obstruction, and are signposted where they leave metalled roads. The duty of local authorities to install signposts extends to the placing of signs along a path or way, but only where the authority considers it necessary to have a signpost or waymark to assist persons unfamiliar with the locality.

The New Access Rights
Access Land
As well as being able to walk on existing rights of way, under the new legislation you now have access to large areas of open land. You can of course continue to use rights of way footpaths to cross this land, but the main difference is that you can now lawfully leave the path and wander at will, but only in areas designated as access land.

Where to Walk
Areas now covered by the new access rights

Countryside Access Charter

Your rights of way are:

- public footpaths – on foot only. Sometimes waymarked in yellow
- bridle-ways – on foot, horseback and pedal cycle. Sometimes waymarked in blue
- byways (usually old roads), most 'roads used as public paths' and, of course, public roads – all traffic has the right of way

Use maps, signs and waymarks to check rights of way. Ordnance Survey Explorer and Landranger maps show most public rights of way

On rights of way you can:

- take a pram, pushchair or wheelchair if practicable
- take a dog (on a lead or under close control)
- take a short route round an illegal obstruction or remove it sufficiently to get past

You have a right to go for recreation to:

- public parks and open spaces – on foot
- most commons near older towns and cities – on foot and sometimes on horseback
- private land where the owner has a formal agreement with the local authority

In addition you can use the following by local or established custom or consent, but ask for advice if you are unsure:

- many areas of open country, such as moorland, fell and coastal areas, especially those in the care of the National Trust, and some commons
- some woods and forests, especially those owned by the Forestry Commission
- country parks and picnic sites
- most beaches
- canal towpaths
- some private paths and tracks Consent sometimes extends to horse-riding and cycling

For your information:

- county councils and London boroughs maintain and record rights of way, and register commons
- obstructions, dangerous animals, harassment and misleading signs on rights of way are illegal and you should report them to the county council
- paths across fields can be ploughed, but must normally be reinstated within two weeks
- landowners can require you to leave land to which you have no right of access
- motor vehicles are normally permitted only on roads, byways and some 'roads used as public paths'

– Access Land – are shown on Ordnance Survey Explorer maps bearing the access land symbol on the front cover.

'Access Land' is shown on Ordnance Survey maps by a light yellow tint surrounded by a pale orange border.

Restrictions

The right to walk on access land may lawfully be restricted by landowners but whatever restrictions are put into place they have no effect on existing rights of way, and you can continue to walk on them.

Dogs

Dogs can be taken on access land, but must be kept on leads of two metres or less between 1 March and 31 July, and at all times where they are near livestock. In addition landowners may impose a ban on all dogs from fields where lambing takes place for up to six weeks in any year.

General Obstructions

If the right of way is blocked and cannot be followed, there is a long standing view that in such circumstances there is a right to deviate, but this cannot be wholly relied on. Use common sense. If you can get round the obstruction without causing damage, do so. If in doubt retreat.

Report obstructions to the local authority and/or the Ramblers..
www.ramblers.org.uk